Praise for From the Middle Passage to Black Lives Matter

"*From the Middle Passage to Black Lives Matter* invites readers to re-examine the history of European discovery and colonization told from outside of the colonial gaze. Marva McClean overcomes the erasure of truth telling, which has censored our participation and influence within history as people of color, via vivid emotional and visual discourse in storytelling that at times can best be described as poetry. Readers are invited back to the time of Nanny of the Maroons, an archetypal figure connecting resistance movements across the Black Atlantic to give birth centuries later to the Civil Rights Movement and now Black Lives Matter as part of her legacy.

"Marva McClean takes us on a journey running throughout the centuries, recounting her own historical consciousness in confronting social inequities across the globe in search of our common human dignity. She makes an urgent call to educators to acknowledge students' funds of knowledge in creating a cultural space within the curriculum that embraces their cultural heroes/heroines in the awareness of their own empowerment, in much the same way feminist freedom fighter Queen Nanny of the Maroons lighted the path of social justice for the author as a young woman growing up in Jamaica. It is a call we must heed."

Marcus Woolombi Waters, Program Director,
Creative and Professional Writing, Griffith University – Gold Coast, Australia

From the Middle Passage
to Black Lives Matter

This book is part of the Peter Lang Education list.
Every volume is peer reviewed and meets
the highest quality standards for content and production.

PETER LANG
New York • Bern • Berlin
Brussels • Vienna • Oxford • Warsaw

Marva McClean

From the Middle Passage to Black Lives Matter

Ancestral Writing as a Pedagogy of Hope

PETER LANG
New York • Bern • Berlin
Brussels • Vienna • Oxford • Warsaw

Library of Congress Cataloging-in-Publication Data

Names: McClean, Marva, author.
Title: From the middle passage to Black Lives Matter:
ancestral writing as a pedagogy of hope / Marva McClean.
Description: New York: Peter Lang, 2019.
Includes bibliographical references and index.
Identifiers: LCCN 2018035839 | ISBN 978-1-4331-5546-8 (hardback: alk. paper)
ISBN 978-1-4331-5547-5 (paperback: alk. paper) | ISBN 978-1-4331-5491-1 (ebook pdf)
ISBN 978-1-4331-5492-8 (epub) | ISBN 978-1-4331-5493-5 (mobi)
Subjects: LCSH: Africans—America—History. | Africans—Civil rights—America—History.
Civil rights movements—America—History. | Africans—History—Study and teaching.
Civil rights movements—Study and teaching. | Social justice—Study and teaching.
Classification: LCC E29.N3 M375 2019 | DDC 970.00496—dc23
LC record available at https://lccn.loc.gov/2018035839
DOI 10.3726/b14564

Bibliographic information published by **Die Deutsche Nationalbibliothek**.
Die Deutsche Nationalbibliothek lists this publication in the "Deutsche
Nationalbibliografie"; detailed bibliographic data are available
on the Internet at http://dnb.d-nb.de/.

CONTENTS

Part III: Viewing the Curriculum Through an Anti-Colonial Lens

ACKNOWLEDGMENTS

If there is a book you want to read that hasn't been written yet, then you must write it.
—Toni Morrison

Preparation for the writing of this book has been taking shape for decades, going as far back as my school days at Excelsior High School in Kingston, Jamaica, where I was nurtured to be a critical thinker who appreciated the roots of her heritage and the wisdom of her ancestors. Throughout my early schooling, our teachers worked to build our historical consciousness about our colonial background, emphasizing the power of our Indigenous heritage; a majority people of African heritage brought from the Motherland through captivity who resisted and rose above colonialism. Our education, they told us, was a tool to read the world, break boundaries, and dare to achieve. I am therefore grateful to my teachers who introduced me to West Indian history and sparked my interest in slavery and emancipation and Nanny of the Maroons in particular. Deep gratitude goes to my sister Charmaine Wade Perry for the engaged discourses she has facilitated on Nanny of the Maroons, offering me guidance and perspective. Dr. Rovan Locke prodded and provoked political interrogation of key ideological standpoints, pushing me to think critically and to examine Nanny through multiple lenses. In more recent times, my colleague Marcus Waters, whom I met at the 2014 Annual Maroon Conference in Jamaica, directed my attention to the ways in which the culture and history of Indigenous people are entangled across the globe and to the continuing disenfranchisement of Aboriginals in their own country in Australia. Our collaborative inquiry has pushed me to expand my worldview on Indigeneity and the innovative ways in which the resistance movement persists across the globe, standing up to the might of neo-colonialism. I owe him a wealth of gratitude.

I am most grateful to my children who have kept me on my toes with an enlightened perspective of the need to be vigilant and safeguard our heritage and ensure that it is passed down through the generations. The hundreds of children I have taught over the years have pushed me to keep in the forefront the need to disrupt the prevailing hegemonic discourses that propel the mega-narrative of European superiority and ignore the magnificent accomplishments of Black and Indigenous people across the globe. These students have remained a stark reminder of the scholar's responsibility to tell the truth; to counter the marginalization of our history and write our story into living history. They reminded me of the need to write this book so that they can read it and be inspired to take action. I am grateful to them.

The Maroons today exert control over their past, including the history of slavery and emancipation in Jamaica and the New World. I am deeply grateful to the conference committee who organized the 2014 Annual Maroon conference and made the meeting of minds possible. It continues to be a most fascinating and inspiring experience to stand on Maroon land, and I am inspired by this legacy and the warrior woman who led them through the most turbulent warfare with the Imperialists in such a manner that harkened the ending of slavery. And so, I seek to tell the story of the resolute, brave, and committed Nanny of the Maroons, 18th-century freedom fighter; a feminist icon for all generations, and write this narrative with deep gratitude.

INTRODUCTION

From their survival of the horrific Middle Passage, through to riots, rebellions, and revolutions on slave plantations, and in more recent times, the courageous resistance against neo-colonialism as expressed through movements such as Black Lives Matter, I am motivated to bring stories of disenfranchised people into the curriculum and incorporate diverse cultures and students' funds of knowledge as material that speaks to how we can engage in protest, resistance, and enduring change.

Born in Jamaica out of the legacy of British colonialism rooted in the Transatlantic slave trade, I self-identify as an Indigenous scholar and question the pervasive failure of Black children, whom I also identify as Indigenous, in schools across the globe. As I examine this historical background with an ethnographic attentiveness to education and its cultural practices, the story of Nanny of the Maroons becomes increasingly important to my identity. It provides a blueprint to guide my path, connecting me to stories of historical empowerment within the African Diaspora.

I first heard the story of Nanny of the Maroons as a child in Jamaica, told to me, my siblings, and cousins by our grandmother as we gathered to tell stories at evening time. This story pointed to the possibilities that can emerge from courageous action. My grandmother told us that almost three centuries ago, Nanny, leader of the Windward Maroons, escaped from slavery and along with her four brothers established a community that today is firmly rooted in our ancestral heritage. Under the leadership of Nanny and her brothers, the Maroons fought a valiant guerilla warfare with such fortitude that the British were forced to sign peace treaties with them, resulting in their sovereign ownership of the land to this day. These warriors challenged the institution of slavery and helped to bring it to an end. Of all the stories she told, this stood out for me as the mighty accomplishments of an ordinary woman who dared. Since then, this story has remained central to my identity. While I cannot claim to be a Maroon, I identify (Gee, 2001) with the fighting spirit of Nanny, whom Jamaicans readily liken to the biblical David. A small, wiry woman who amassed the meagre resources of her community to thwart the Goliath of Imperialism. I have carried this story around with me, plucking courage from the metaphor, applying the message it upholds as a blueprint for my professional development.

While colonial narratives portrayed and simplified Nanny as a flat figure by calling her "obeah woman" and "old hag" in the few places she is mentioned, the oral history carried over the ages and post-colonial texts by Caribbean scholars reveal Nanny as complex and multi-faceted with contradictory subjectivities and desires. It is this perspective that I convey in my scholarship. The story of Nanny's indomitable will, her efforts and success in carving out an alternative society in Nanny Town, and her perseverance in fighting the British to earn the identity of a thorn in their side, all speak to the will of any marginalized or disenfranchised people who are determined to confront adversity and assert their rights. Based on the relevance of Nanny of the Maroons in my personal story and cultural heritage, I am committed to taking agentive action to assert her biography, and in so doing, directly address the paucity of the stories of rebel leaders such as her in the historiography of slavery and resistance movements. I ask myself, if her story has had such an impact on my life, how might children be affected when they are denied the opportunity to experience similar stories from their cultural heritage in their academic lives?

The writing, sharing, and asserting of these stories must be a deliberate act of conscientization to confront and disrupt the Western world's attempt to effect the erasure of Indigenous people and their cultures from contemporary history. The legitimation of cultural capital of marginalized groups is essential to the conscientization of the curriculum that social justice educators seek. According to Freire (1970), conscientization is an act of understanding that allows the oppressed to identify the unequal power and resource distribution that exist and to devise the means by which to transform an oppressive reality into an empowering experience. Freire's (1998) work calls attention to the potential of educators to create and nurture transformative educational experiences that resist the confines of dominant paradigms. This is a channel to assist children to share and bring alive their own cultural stories as a method of pushing against pedagogical limitations in the classroom, pointing educators to ways in which to answer the question: *How are the children doing?* This popular greeting from the peoples of the African continent pushes me into a stance of criticality as I ponder this persistent failure of our children in school.

I have long been concerned with the deficit framings of stories and the history of Indigenous people in classroom texts which do not address the larger systemic issues that shape the contemporary lives of children. It is important to examine those situations where the texts that include stories of people of color utilize a deficit frame, and more often than not, present them in roles such as laborers, victims, criminals, and maids. I have borne witness to the debilitating impact on children of color in classrooms where their background is presented in this one-dimensional way; where race and ethnicity are constructed along lines of superiority and inferiority. In contexts where the emotional dimensions of literacy are ignored, I have seen children cringe and diminish. In contrast, where I have utilized the critical tradition to engage children as curriculum collaborators, I have observed that storytelling provides strength for Indigenous children in classrooms, as it did for me. I remember the fragility of my own position in Western classrooms extending all the way to the academy, and I offer my experiences as guiding principles to validate the cultural life of our offspring, engage their stories as cultural spaces, and lift up their voices in acknowledgment that they have a historical and cultural background that is valid, substantial, and of great merit.

It is empowering for both student and teacher when these stories are relocated within contemporary experiences taking place in local communities and classrooms. These stories have the potential to become significant guideposts for ways in which the fight and resistance against slavery may parallel the experiences that youth face with discrimination and police brutality in our time today. In particular, they highlight that disenfranchisement is not a permanent state; it can be confronted and overcome in creative ways. Scholars exploring the artistry of storytelling emphasize the power of story in addressing the fragility of the human psyche; its power to explore that tender space within that can lead to transforming the lives of children (Estes, 1992; Whyte, 1994). Knowing as I do that literacy practices promote worldviews and political ideologies, I come face to face with the question: *How do we disrupt the pervasive narrative of oppression and tell the world and our children the truth?*

Storytelling then becomes one of the most significant tools I use to translate my ideology into practice. And it is the story of Nanny of the Maroons that I share with the world. In this narrative, rooted in auto-ethnography, I emphasize how the story of Nanny of the Maroons has influenced my life and assisted me in crafting an ideological perspective in facing the inequity that typifies the world in which I live. I make connections to the colonial past world of Indigenous people traumatized by oppression, to our contemporary world where people of color continue to be traumatized by new forms of oppression. And I emphasize the imaginative and radical forms of our enduring resistance going back to the era of slavery through to the Civil Rights Movement and Black Lives Matter.

Based on my understanding and relationship to my heritage I know that these stories and the memories and mythologies of archetypes such as Nanny can contribute to embracing our children into the classrooms in schools and in their communities. This is an important step to internationalize the curriculum, investigate the world, and recognize and honor the perspectives of others. This, I believe, will honor our common humanity and improve the education of Indigenous children across the globe. The United Nation 2009 *State of the World's Indigenous Peoples* Address (p.6) asserts that "indigenous people continue to suffer discrimination, marginalization, extreme poverty and conflict." The forum confirms that worldwide, Indigenous peoples suffer from lower levels of education than their non-Indigenous counterparts. This contemporary situation can be directly traced back to the ideology asserted during the so-called Age of Discovery, whereby the Catholic Church assumed the right to claim the land and resources of people they considered to be inferior. Slavery, colonization, and the seizure of ancestral land resulted from this ideology, the residual effects of which continue to oppress Indigenous people, often depriving them of their land, languages, practices, and worldviews.

This hegemonic perspective has prevailed and remains deeply entrenched in the policies and culture of most post-colonial and neo-colonial societies. It is an ideology that seeks to negate the validity of our story; historical truths that are left out of the mega-narratives written from a Eurocentric worldview vested in this falsely constructed intellectual perspective. In the USA, this perspective has led to the dislocation of Native Americans from their sacred land, resulting in poverty and social ills on reservations in the 21st century. Across the globe, in Australia, Aboriginal people have been forcibly removed from their ancestral land as large mining companies seek to expand their profits. In the United States, African Americans routinely experience brutality due to racial profiling and police aggression, and many of the children are failing in school. Stories of the historical empowerment of Indigenous people are powerful tools to disrupt this hegemonic stance. I hold myself accountable to do so.

I accept that of necessity, I must expose my inner self in order to share with the world and position the value of Indigenous heritage as classroom pedagogy. How I define and understand myself is inextricably tied to how I conduct my professional work and navigate myself through the world. While I recognize that some readers may feel uncomfortable with the critical perspective and the anti-colonial ideology expressed in this text (Ellis & Flaherty, 1992, p. 3), I am deliberate in revealing my subjectivities and assert that research is subjective and contextual as well as it may be empirical, that people who have suffered are often in a unique position to give voice to the suffering of others. Through my personal story, I assert that Indigenous Knowledge Production (Waters, 2012) provides a broad landscape for educators to investigate and access material that will extend their capacity to address the needs of the diverse student population that inhabits their classrooms, extending from grade school through to higher education. Indigenous Knowledge Production offers a narrative that opens up a portal into the investigation of the gifts that Indigenous people bring to the classroom and to the academy: a history of colonization and a concern with telling the truth from our perspective outside of/and in addition to the canons of Eurocentric literature.

In utilizing the analytical and investigative lens of social justice I assert stories/narratives from Indigenous cultures that center on the cultural retentions and the heroism of ordinary people to stand up to injustice and change the conditions of their lives and their people. I wish to contribute to the global discourse on how historical, local, and social political processes influence the lives of children of color, often depriving them of an equitable education and a fair chance of success in the society. Through examples of my lived experience in practice, I assert specific strategies to disrupt this and replace it with socially just pedagogy. In keeping with the radical imaginary of Indigenous resistance, I write to insist that the world takes the history of disenfranchised people and their interconnectedness as seriously as I do.

Intrigued by Nanny's achievements as a resistance leader and rebel who refused to give in to the forces of oppression, I have claimed her as essential to my cultural identity and seek to critically examine the empowering impact her story has had on the historical and political consciousness that has shaped my path as a social-justice educator. In response to the exclusion of warriors of justice such as Nanny from mainstream curriculum across the globe, I confront and work to intentionally disrupt the meta-narrative written from the Eurocentric perspective where Black people were brought to the new world as slaves who succumbed to servitude and later were emancipated through the benevolence of the White man. Not only has this process been interesting, it has also been liberating and empowering.

This book is an act of telling the children the truth, of seeking a place in the curriculum which highlights and honors the courage and achievements of Indigenous warriors and asserts storytelling as pedagogy that builds students' capacity to interpret, synthesize, and apply their learning in school to real-life situations. Working in both formal and informal educational settings and community spaces, I have engaged in a collaborative process with my students towards establishing a community grounded in the tenets of socio-cultural theory (Gee, 2001; Gonzalez, Moll, & Amanti, 2005). In this space I enact the fragile positioning of the researcher—exploring one's subjectivities in an effort to build trust and understanding between my students and me to ensure their access to a space in which to articulate and write their own cultural narratives. This continuous self-study has enabled me to utilize my life story as texts incorporated into my practice as I engage in live research and interactive process in middle school classrooms in south Florida. Here, my students experience first-hand my professional development as an educator and my evolving research on Maroonage and Indigeniety. Asserting education as a continuous, pervasive experience, I share field notes with them and involve them in the process of securing and utilizing primary source data that accesses the imaginative rendering of the critical tradition focused on Indigenous perspectives. Collaboratively, we expand the curriculum to include students' cultural background, their life stories, and themes such as the Civil Rights Movement, International Women's History, Black Lives Matter, and global cultures, incorporating the Web as tools of inquiry. Within this context, the students see me as a learner engaged in teaching, learning, and discovery; a context which positions them as experts and producers of texts, elevating them above the traditional identity of student (learner), eschewing the notion of tabula rasa.

The cultural storylines that have played a pivotal role in framing my identity are privileged in this text as I assert my interpretation of the struggles and adversities that challenged my ancestors and the creativity with which they tackled adversity (Holman Jones, 2004). As Jenny Sharpe (2003) articulated, "Slavery continues to haunt the present because its stories have been improperly buried" (xi). Storytelling is a route to survival. The rich legacy of Nanny, African freedom fighter, should be brought to the awareness of children and educators worldwide as an example of the possibilities that life has to offer when one perseveres and fights against injustice. As I retrieve Nanny's story from the annals of history, I am particularly interested in bringing to the academic community alternative ways of crafting pedagogy, and bringing student voices, their background and cultural heritage, into the curriculum. Not only will this add to the discourse on social justice and equity, it will also bring critical considerations to preparing educators to achieve educational justice through innovative experiences such as fieldwork in post-colonial nations and underserved school communities, engaging students as knowledge producers and critics in the classroom.

To fail to teach the meaning of stories such as Nanny's to students of color is to deny them access to their cultural heritage, to deprive them of a significant portion of the legacy that binds them together and makes them part of a cultural identity rather than alienated individuals scattered in classrooms across the USA and the globe.

I believe that we can use stories to offer hope when cases rooted in racial prejudice and discrimination such as those of Eric Garner, Trayvon Martin, and Tamir Rice arise. I am interested in the inclusion of Nanny of the Maroons in the textbooks and literature of the Caribbean and North America, where a large percentage of children of African descent reside. Storytelling draws on a broad range of human activity that addresses issues of survival, creativity, and perseverance. It is particularly important to Indigenous people because of its orality and the central role it has played in the survival of their heritage despite imperialism and the continued onslaught of neo-colonialism. Scholars working in the fields of storytelling (Estes, 1992) and rites of passage theory have articulated the significant ways in which cultural narratives have worked to support and uplift children who have experienced alienation and dislocation.

Organization of the Book

The book is organized in three parts with 10 chapters. There are three chapters in Part I, five in Part II and two in Part III.

I apply a qualitative theoretical approach, drawing on critical literacy frames including socio-cultural theory, auto-ethnography, and third space theories to examine the specific conceptual notion of Nanny of the Maroons as a warrior of justice aligned with the 21st-century critical perspective as articulated by scholars such as Peter McLaren, Gloria Ladson-Billings, Ira Bogotch, Henry Giroux, and Geneva Gay. In presenting this experiential understanding of history fostered by colonialism/neo-colonialism, I utilize the story as the framework to investigate the globalization of education and to assert the cultural capital of Indigenous people coming from a variety of racial and ethnic backgrounds including Africa, the Caribbean, North America, and Australia and argue that stories from these regions can be used as curriculum resource.

Part I: Reading the Curriculum Through a Post-Colonial Lens

This section examines how an educator's biography may influence her practice and the implications for culturally relevant pedagogy in schools across the globe. Peering through the lens of auto-ethnicity, I investigate the way Nanny of the Maroons shaped my identity as a young child in Jamaica and discuss in general the value of having heroes from one's culture as role models to guide one's development.

Part II: Reading the Curriculum Through Global Inquiry

In asserting Kessler's (2000) view that the classroom should be a "place where the heart is safe and the soul welcomed" (p. 16), I share specific methods I have used to build students' academic identity, engaging them as knowledge producers and cultural critics in the classroom. In this section of the book, written in five chapters, I examine how I have privileged the story of Nanny of the Maroons in my classroom as pivotal to the thrust to create a shared space that leads to the fostering of meaningful relationships that acknowledge and honor diversity. It demonstrates how I have taken the developing research on Maroon communities in Jamaica to middle school classrooms in the United States, engaging students as active participants in a program of global awareness. Further, the investigation into the role of culture in education is extended to the Aboriginal First Nation culture of Australia, drawing parallels not only with Maroon culture, but also with other cultures such as Native Americans and Jewish Americans: groups that have historically experienced disenfranchisement. Students' writing samples are privileged as authentic and valid texts asserting their role as knowledge producers and critics of literature.

Part III: Viewing the Curriculum Through an Anti-Colonial Lens

In this section of the book I support the scholarship that building a community of practice uproots the notion of the erasure of Indigenous people as it investigates the way Nanny and the Maroons of Jamaica courageously forged a community of practice harkening back hundreds of years to the people's African roots. The role of the land in rooting Maroon culture is examined in a society that remains self-governing, sustainable, and politically autonomous. This section also draws comparison with other Indigenous cultures such as the Aboriginals of Australia, the Native Americans of the United States and Canada, and African American children in the United States. This book recommends the Maroon community as an example for other Indigenous cultures struggling for survival.

At the end of each chapter there is a set of synthesis questions which are designed to provoke a reflection of key concepts explored in the chapter and invite a conversation with others, especially conversations between intergenerational groups. They are especially intended to spark conversations with youth, and are envisioned as possible writing prompts or a way to kick off research in school and community programs. Youth may be guided to make generalizations about the meaning, significance, or value of the material and then apply what has been gleaned to the larger social, cultural, ethical, or political context in which they are located. For example, reference is made to the Black Lives Matter movement in the United States and the plight of the Aboriginals of Australia, providing an opportunity for an investigation into the socio-political context of each group.

All three sections include chapters which investigate how Nanny's extraordinary pattern of behavior became the impetus for a people to be resistant to boundaries and subjugation and persevere to overcome and thrive. Nanny has provided me with an opportunity to explore and critique creative and culturally relevant practices in schools. In this book I emphasize the importance of encouraging children and providing them with the space to talk about their culture, to attain visibility and have their voices heard. Within this context, the classroom becomes a space for cultural validation, identity formation, and academic achievement. The samples of narrative products created by students and the elevation of their voices in classroom discourse emphasize the value of placing them at the center of classroom pedagogy where they become expert knowledge producers (Saavedra, 2011).

My motivation in writing this text is shaped by the need to move beyond the notion of a post-colonial world and bring to life the complexities inherent in the thrust for the civil rights of people of color within the neo-colonialist state of the 21st century. This book is neither a historical account nor an empirical study; rather, it is a theoretical/autobiographical text concerned with the socio-cultural dynamics of Maroonage and its enduring influence upon present-day Jamaica and individuals such as me.

This book will provide readers with an opportunity to extend their global perspectives about characters and people beyond their own communities and articulate the role of culture in their own everyday lives. It affirms the central role of storytelling in academic life and community building.

I hope that through the writing of these chapters I am making a vital contribution to the planting of truthful seeds about the people of African descent in the Americas; about Indigenous people across the globe. It is my hope that as they are planted, these seeds will take root, flourish, and blossom into wonderful fruits that will nourish our intellect as much as they will our soul.

References

Ellis, C., & Flaherty, M. G. (1992). *Investigating subjectivities*. Newbury Park, CA: Sage.

Estes, C. P. (1992). *Women who run with the wolves: Myths & legends of the wild woman archetype*. New York, NY: Ballantine Books.

Freire, P. (1970/2007). *Pedagogy of the oppressed*. New York, NY: Continuum.

Freire, P. (1998). *Pedagogy of freedom: Ethics, democracy & civic courage*. Lanham, MD: Rowman & Littlefield.

Gee, P. A. (2001). Identity as an analytic lens for research in education. *Review of Research in Education, 25*, 99–125.

Gonzalez, N., Moll, L. C., & Amanti, C. (2005). *Funds of knowledge: Theorizing practices in households and classrooms*. Newark, NJ: Lawrence Erlbaum.

Holman Jones, S. (2004). Building connections in qualitative research. Carolyn Ellis and Art Bochner in conversation with Stacy Holman Jones. *Forum: Qualitative Social Research, 5*(3). Retrieved from http://www.qualitative-research.net/index.php/fqs/article/view/552/1194

Kessler, R. (2000). *The soul of education. Helping students find connection, compassion, and character at school.* Alexandria, VA: ASCD.

Saavedra, M. (2011). Language & literacy in the borderlands: Acting upon the world through testimonies. *Language Arts, 88*(4), 261–269.

Sharpe, J. (2003). *The ghosts of slavery: A literary archeology of black women's lives.* Minneapolis, MN: University of Minnesota Press.

United Nations State of Indigenous People Address. (2009). https:www.un.org/esa/spcdev/unpfii/documents/SOWIP/en/SOWIP_web.pdf

Waters, M. (2012). *Contemporary urban indigenous "dreamings": Interaction, engagement and creative practice* (PhD thesis). Griffith University, Brisbane, Australia. Retrieved from https://www120.secure.griffith.edu.au/rch/file/e2e82d05-3f75-bd70-8602-89f06b4e6e9b/1/Waters_2012_02Thesis.pdf

Whyte, D. (1994). *The heart aroused: Poetry & the preservation of the soul in corporate America.* New York, NY: Currency Doubleday.

PART I
READING THE CURRICULUM
THROUGH A POST-COLONIAL LENS

PREAMBLE TO PART I: READING THE CURRICULUM THROUGH A POST-COLONIAL LENS

Shadows of the Past (Exploring Subjectivities)

Columbus' arrival in Xyamaca opened up Jamaica—once a country peacefully occupied by the Tainos, a tribe of the Arawak Indians—as part of the New World, changing not only the geography but also the social and political landscape. In keeping with the philosophy expressed in the Age of Discovery, Columbus claimed this *New World* for Spain, even as the people welcomed him, offering their generosity. He commented that the Indians were so gracious and trusting that he could easily capture them with 50 of his men. He observed their gentle nature, characterized by friendliness, and their lifestyle, governed by a strong connection to the land and water within an organized community centered around the cacique. Historical records from conquistadores, professional Spanish warriors, reveal that the native people traded with them: "they gave us everything they had. They are very gentle and without knowledge of evil" (The Tainos, 2014). Columbus seized the land in the name of Spain, and by the 16th century the institution of slavery, initiated in the region earlier by the Portuguese, was developing into an enterprise that would soon dominate the political, cultural, and ecological landscape of the region.

Michael Dorris' book *Morning Girl* (1994/1999) brings alive the eco-Indigenous lifestyle of the Arawaks in Hispaniola prior to the arrival of Columbus. It is a story I have integrated into the curriculum I use with middle school students as a conscious attempt to confront and disrupt the perspective of Native people being deficient and to emphasize the rich content of their culture and its enduring legacy. I find it particularly useful to explore concepts of identity engendered through one's racial and cultural heritage. The protagonist, Morning Girl, whose society has no mirrors, sees her reflection in the river that runs through her village. When she questions her parents about her appearance, they guide her to see the beauty of her features by making comparisons with the natural environment around her, noting the similarity of her face to the roundness of the yams they eat and the brown hue of her complexion to the shades of the sand bed. It is Morning Girl who witnesses the arrival of Columbus' ships along the seascape moving towards her village, and the reader experiences a sharp anticipation as to the impending consequences of this development when two different worlds collide, two different perspectives clash, and hegemonic power seeks to acquire material resources at all cost over the cultural richness of a people and their sovereign rights to their ethnic and geo-political identity. Thus, the Spanish intrusion on the native land precipitated a system of exploitation of the land and human resources. The Spanish ruled Jamaica from 1494–1655, resulting in a near genocide of the Tainos/Arawaks (Jamaica National Heritage Trust, 2014).

The history that developed from this interaction has been recorded by the White settlers who wrote in a manner to advance their perspective. Beginning with the Spanish conquistadores and extending to the British colonialists, supporters of the inhumane slavery society sought to justify their commodification of human beings. Consequently, these records are written from the perspective of the settler colonialist with little or no acknowledgment of the culture and the contributions of the Indigenous people, including those forcibly brought onto the plantocracy and those native to the lands now identified as the New World. This was in fact a world new to Europeans, who had no knowledge of its prior history, as is evidenced by Columbus' assumption that he had landed somewhere in Asia.

The First Colonial Empire in the New World

The Spaniards in Hispaniola imported slaves as early as 1510, and by the middle of the 16th century, Spain had founded the first colonial empire in the Americas and Black people were being imported as slaves from the African continent as labor for the estates in substitute for the Native people who were being decimated by the diseases the Europeans brought and the cruel inhumane treatment at their hands. At first the number of enslaved Africans taken was small. In about 1650, however, with the development of plantations on the newly colonized Caribbean islands and American mainland, the trade grew. Old World diseases such as smallpox, flu, and typhus decimated much of the native population. Augier, Gordon, Hall, & Reckord (1960) emphasized that while there were free people on the island, they shunned wage labor, and it was cheaper to acquire an African slave than a European laborer (p. 46).

As the islands developed into sites of economic power, so did enmity and war over them. Britain set its eyes on Jamaica and war ensued with the Spanish. In 1655 the British finally overpowered the Spanish at Rio Nuevo in St. Mary, Jamaica, a site that sits in the neighborhood where my family resides. As the Spanish fled, they freed the slaves so that the British would not have them. These slaves escaped into the mountains along with the remaining Native Americans, setting in motion the forging of Maroon societies.

A Terrible Trade: The Development of the Slave Trade and Slavery

On the continent of Africa, Africans were collected by small coastal tribes carrying out raids against the people. They captured men, women, and children and then sold them into slavery where they were transported to the Americas via the Middle Passage.

> The journey between Africa and the Americas, The Middle Passage, could take four to six weeks, but the average lasted between two and three months. Chained and crowded with no room to move, Africans were forced to make the journey under terrible conditions, naked and lying in filth.
>
> In the 360 years between 1500 and the end of the slave trade in the 1860s, at least 12 million Africans were forcibly taken to the Americas—then known as the New World to European settlers. This largest forced migration in human history relocated some 50 ethnic and linguistic groups (Gates, 2015).

It is estimated that 1.5 to 2 million men, women, and children died en route on the Middle Passage. While it is a fact that many African tribes captured and sold their enemies into the Atlantic slave trade, it is also a fact that many African leaders, including Abd al Qadir of Senegal and King Afonso of Kongo, resisted the slave trade and engaged in many strategies to protect their communities and deter Western imposition on the continent.

According to reports, slavery began in what is now the United States of America (USA) when a ship brought 20 Africans, including three women, initiating the brutal system of human bondage. It is stated that around 1619 a slave ship entered the USA through the Atlantic Ocean and across the James River into Virginia (Keenan, 2002). Over 40% of Africans entered the US through the port city of Charleston, South Carolina, the center of the US slave trade. By the middle of the 19th century, the southern states were providing two thirds of the world's supply of cotton. While cotton cultivation developed in North America, sugar became the most profitable cultivation in the Caribbean region during the 18th century.

Life on the Sugar Plantation

"The struggle to dominate others is as old as society" (Gonzalez, Houston, & Chen, 2000, p. xxii). Britain's trading of Black people from Africa developed and expanded in tandem with the country's thrust to become a global entity, an economic super power, and an empire where the sun never set. The Whites brought with them the barbaric and savage methods of leadership, underlined by a philosophy of racial and social superiority, started centuries before under King Alfred the Great. In 16th-century Britain, society was organized along strong social stratification of superiority and inferiority. Punishment was harsh and savage, as exemplified by the systems of torture, quartering, and execution that governed the social and political organization of Britain during this time. The presiding leaders, including governors and superintendents in the island of Jamaica during slavery, operated with harshness and inhumanity in keeping with this background. On the plantations, the planters also practiced savage barbarism that reflected this kind of orientation. As sugar production developed in Jamaica, slavery was established as the dominant economic organization and racism was created through forced immigration of the African people and the movement to subjugate them by taking away their identity, their culture, and their rituals. And alongside that, resistance was initiated and enacted and maintained.

The Development of Maroon Communities

Descendants of runaway slaves who first fled to the interior mountains of Jamaica after the Spanish abdicated to the British in 1655, the Maroons gathered strength throughout the years and organized into a political and military force with the subsequent leadership of Nanny in the late 17th and early 18th centuries, along with her brothers, who were equally stalwart in guerilla warfare and political organization. Jamaican folklore states that Nanny and her brothers were captured together and brought to Jamaica, their father being a military leader of Koromantyn heritage, an Ashante from the Gold Coast (Ghana). This ties in with the story that asserts her royal lineage as a source which ignited and nurtured her agency for freedom.

Nanny and her brothers established villages which remain today in the almost inaccessible interior of the island; autonomous communities which breathe with the life of the indomitable will of a people who continue to honor their African ancestral roots. Nanny's history becomes an exploration into freedom, integrity, and perseverance and speaks to the influence of historical processes on the lives of women and the communities to which they belong. In the early 18th century, Nanny settled in the Cockpit of the Blue Mountain terrain and set about becoming a troubling force to the British Empire. Through her inspiring leadership she attracted freedom fighters to the hills of Jamaica at a site later named Nanny Town, and built up a fierce guerilla army, schooled in the intimate terrains of the land, and subverted and thwarted the colonial forces of the British army. At the same time, her brothers established communities throughout the western and northern interior of the island to enact subterfuge against the British in defiance of slavery.

Mapping the dense forests and mountainous terrains, the Maroons utilized spatial schemas, landmarks, and pathways, tapping into the spiritual terrains of non-linear time, to access the liminal world of their ancient heritage and succor the strength to feed and sustain them in battle against the colonial forces. For over 30 years Nanny freed more than 800 slaves and helped them to resettle in the Maroon community. As stories of her courageous feats traveled throughout the land the oppressed were inspired and Nanny's reputation elevated her to the standing of a folk hero. There were stories of British attacks on Nanny Town, but thanks to the strategic location and her idea of having only one entrance/exit to the town, they were able to fight off the British soldiers even though they were severely outnumbered. In staying the course, in continuing in the journey of the heroine, her actions resulted in the weakening of the force of Imperialism. Robinson (1993) cited a report of the 1733 legislature that said that the Maroons

> plundered all around them, and caused several plantations to be thrown up and abandoned, and prevented many valuable tracts of land from being cultivated, to the great prejudice and diminution of His Majesty's revenue, as well as trade, navigation and consumption of British manufacturers; and to the manifest weakening and preventing the further increase of the strength and inhabitants in the island. (p. 48)

The British were so flummoxed by the relentless assault of the Maroons that they negotiated a peace treaty with Cudjoe in 1739. It is well noted that Nanny was against the signing of peace treaties because she felt it compromised the Maroons' stance against Imperialism. However, she went along with the consensus of her brothers, the other Maroon leaders. Today, Maroon identity is rooted in the assurance of their warrior spirit and the knowledge that they fought valiantly for their freedom and inspired others to stand up to the giant of Imperialism. I believe that enriching the curriculum with heroes from the culture of people of color such as Nanny of the Maroons will serve as an effective educational tool that encourages participants to imagine new perspectives and provide students with alternative visions of possibilities, and to:

- enrich the academic experience of children of color and white children alike.
- confirm our common humanity.

Like any community of practice, the Maroon communities of Jamaica are not without conflict and problems, and I wish to assert that I am not essentializing them as a romantic pastoral community that is conflict free. However, they are a distinct contrast to the harsh, oppressive landscape that many diverse people inhabit in the concrete jungles of the developing world and in places such as urban centers occupied by Aboriginals in Australia, for example. In addition, in asserting the Maroon community as an example of Indigenous people thriving in the ancestral wisdom of their Afrocentric heritage, I share the ways in which they have maintained centuries-old rituals within a contemporary society and I evaluate their social organization on their own terms, careful to not use measurement of, or standards such as, per capita income or those that are used in developed countries such as the USA where I reside. And as I give consideration to the turbulence that exists in communities across the globe, there are certain defining features that stand out. The Maroon communities of Jamaica provide examples of Indigenous people maintaining a creative relationship with the local environments, demonstrating diversity and multilayered thinking. This relationship also enables intergenerational teaching practices between elders and youth, facilitating the survival of age-old traditions. The continued survival of these communities references the historical, political, and cultural forces that inform and shape Indigeneity and makes a significant contribution to Indigenous Knowledge Production.

From my locally rooted understanding of the global impact of colonization and slavery, I trace and connect Indigenous Knowledge back to the roots of African ancestry, connecting it to the Kamilaroi Aboriginal Dreaming of Australia, Maroon society in Suriname, for example, and the diverse children of various global ethnicities whom I have taught over the years and continue to interact with today. Central to Indigenous Knowledge Production is the philosophy that communal living and intellectual and spiritual leadership by elders were, and remain, a pivotal force in the fostering of communities of practice. In subsequent chapters I share how storytelling has energized my classrooms. Students bring their cultural stories into the classroom and together we explore how heroes and heroines from all over the globe utilized strategies buoyed by their character traits to face injustice and prevail. As our common human heritage emerges it soon becomes clear how we are all connected across the globe. It emerges as an excellent tool to create historical awareness and emphasize to students the role they must play as agents of change in this chaotic world.

I believe that incorporating pedagogy rooted in Indigenous Knowledge Production will help to ground Indigenous children in the classroom environment and promote their academic achievement. This will directly address social injustice and inequity in schools across the globe. And, as Freire (1970/1990) asserted, it will provide the opportunity to honor the voice of the powerless with a pedagogy of hope.

In chapters 1–3 I reflect on how my identity has been shaped by the conceptualization of Nanny of the Maroons as a heroine who speaks from the past to the fragile and developing persona of the Jamaican girl whose emerging identity is shaped by the colorful and powerful stories passed down through the oral tradition of her family and her community. I explore how orality works to influence the shaping of identity—or self—in response to personal and physical changes that are connected to historical events. I then trace the subjective process experienced in a lived event influenced by the cultural and geographic environment of the Maroon communities in Jamaica. I emphasize how the powerful histories of Indigenous peoples explored through storytelling and memory-making reveal the complex interactions between the multiple, and often divergent, perspectives of the tellers of that story. This text asserts the significant role that culture plays in shaping memory as it explores the interface between memory and history, cultural identity and race.

References

Augier, F. R., Gordon, S. C., Hall, D. G., & Reckord, M. (1960). *The making of the West Indies*. London, England: Longmans, Green & Company.

Dorris, M. (1994/1999). *Morning girl*. New York, NY: Hyperion.

Freire, P. (1970/2007). *Pedagogy of the oppressed*. New York, NY: Continuum.

Gates, H. L. Jr. (2015). The African American migration story: Many rivers to cross. PBS. http://.pbs.org/wnet/african-americans-many-rivers-to-cross/history/on-african-american-migrations/

Gonzalez, A., Houston, M., & Chen, V. (2000). *Our voices: Essays in culture, ethnicity, and communication*. Los Angeles, CA: Roxbury.

Jamaica National Heritage Trust. (2014). Retrieved from www.jnht.com/index.php

Keenan, S. (2002). *Scholastic encyclopedia of women in the United States*. New York, NY. Scholastic.

Robinson, C. (1993). *The iron thorn: The defeat of the British by the Jamaican Maroons*. Kingston, Jamaica: LMH.

The Tainos. Retrieved from https://www.tumblr.com/search/native%20

· 1 ·

ROOTING IDENTITY

Individual Memory and the Collective Narrative

Who we are is mirrored back to us and announced to the world by the symbols we surround ourselves with.

—Dr. Alberto Villoldo, *Courageous Dreaming*

As descendants of African heritage, oral history is vital to our very existence. We know that not all history is written in books. Much of our history has been stored in the minds of our people who lived it and passed it down throughout the generations by word of mouth and symbolic artifacts. For thousands of years people have passed on their memories by telling and retelling them. As a young girl growing up in Jamaica, my mother, aunts, and grandmother in particular shaped my upbringing through the stories they told us. My fragile emerging identity was buttressed by the examples of perseverance and heroism in the stories they told, and in particular, that of Nanny of the Maroons. These stories not only recalled our history and family life but they also presented us with guidelines for existing in the world. This storytelling was centrally rooted within a radical imaginary that nurtured a disenfranchised community to use cultural production to overcome oppression and inequity.

The memory rises in my mind as if it were yesterday. I was the 8-year-old narrator of the play on the Morant Bay rebellion put on at Oracabessa

Primary School. Along with my peers, I dramatized Paul Bogle's (one of Jamaica's national heroes, killed by Governor Eyre in 1865) militant march into Morant Bay where he stood up to the governor and demanded that the rights of his people be recognized, etching into the national identity one of the most significant rebellions in the island's history. While this dramatic story about Paul Bogle captured my attention as a significant one among the collections within our archival memory, it was the other hero(ine), the female one, who caught my attention and held me spellbound. This annual performance paved the road to my discovery of, and relationship with, Nanny of the Maroons, who soon became a focal point in my emerging identity.

The Terror of the Maroons

During my youth in school in Jamaica, Nanny and our cultural warriors such as Bogle and Marcus Garvey were a staple in our classroom pedagogy, presented to us by our parents and teachers as examples of our country's fighting spirit and perseverance worthy of emulation. For a young developing country, it was important that we identified with heroes who provided us with a blueprint for productive living. Nanny was special as a female warrior who led the freedom movement in the Blue Mountains of Jamaica in such a manner that she became known as the thorn in the side of the British. For an impressionable child like me, in love with the beauty of language, this metaphor resonated. In time, this fearsome, Black Ashante warrior, female epitome of power, became for me the archetype of the Jamaican personae, and a mythic representation of myself.

A member of the Ashanti Tribe, Queen Nanny is presumed to have been born around the 1680s in Africa's Gold Coast (now known as Ghana) and to have arrived in Jamaica around the 1700s. Her time of death is estimated to have been 1755. The Maroon community esteemed Nanny and bestowed upon her the identity of Queen Mother, a translation of the Koromante, Hni. This title has maintained its cultural significance and political agency throughout the years, and within this era, it is symbolic of agency and transformation within Jamaica and throughout the African Diaspora. Shepherd, Bereton, and Bailey (1995) referred to her as a historical woman who could not be ignored. Jamaica's past and only female prime minister, Portia Simpson, often spoke of the spirit of Nanny when addressing the people of Jamaica (Simpson, 2014).

The rebel fighters acquired the name Maroon within a system whose vocabulary sought to inflict on them an identity that their very resistance rejected. The word *maroon* is said to have been derived from the Spanish *cimarron*, meaning wild and untamed, which was originally used as a descriptor for wild or runaway animals and on plantations where African/Black people were inventoried as part of the livestock. Sharpe (2003) noted that this was deliberate, part of the methodology of attempting to dehumanize Black people in the New World. It is one that bears connection to the historically heinous word, nigger, as used in the United States to denigrate African Americans.

The steep inclines and curvaceous landscape of the Blue Mountain territory welcomed the determined warriors and seemed to shield them within the deep folds of its thickly forested slopes. Nanny's brother Cudjoe found solace and protection in the rugged limestone plateau of the Cockpit Country, where he established Cudjoe Town; nearby, another brother, Accompong, set up Accompong Town in the interior folds of St. Elizabeth. In keeping with the creative agency of Black people, the rebels did not succumb to the bureaucratic identity or use of pejorative terminology, but went on to assert their right to freedom and gave the Empire such a fight as to reduce the authority of slavery in the island. "Existing as autonomous pockets of resistance, the Maroons conducted raids on the surrounding plantations, ever increasing their numbers with new runaways" (Sharpe, 2003, p. 5).

Rucker (2015) emphasized that "Nothing is further from the truth than the popular belief that the African in the New World was in love with slavery and succumbed calmly to it. The fact is that he rebelled against it from the United States to Argentina without number" (p. 222). Robinson (1993) noted, "A disheartened Governor Hunter wrote home to say that: The terror of them spreads itself everywhere" (pp. 48–49).

A Thorn in Their Side

Folklore suggests that Nanny was descended from royal blood and possessed a demeanor of self-assurance and leadership. Instead of settling into a life of servitude when she arrived aboard a slaver in Jamaica, she set her sights on the mountainous terrain and escaped into the interior to become a fierce freedom fighter intent on pushing back against the tyranny of slavery.

As the legend goes, Nanny marched deep into the heart of Jamaican Blue Mountain territory and immediately began to establish a community of practice centered on freedom and resistance to tyranny. She garnered weapons from the objects around until she and her people were eventually able to confiscate weapons from the enemy when they dared to venture into the interior. Rebel ex-slaves who escaped into the mountains joined Nanny's band to become members of the Windward Maroons. Empowered and determined, she confronted limitations that socially organized women into stereotypical categories, leading and fighting alongside her brothers. Her four brothers assembled similar groups along the island's interior to form the Leeward Maroons, and the groups courageously engaged the British in warfare which led to the signing of peace treaties in 1739. This resulted in the Maroons gaining sovereignty over the land, which remains in their possession to this day. At the time, the Maroons negotiated for conditions that would enable them to maintain a livelihood. For example, the Articles of Pacification signed by both Leeward and Windward Maroons state that Maroon women could apply for licenses in order to sell their hogs, fowls, and any other kind of stock or provisions in public markets.

These stories, which acknowledge and celebrate the fighting spirit of our African ancestors, were the substance of my classroom experience. Miss Parker, my elementary school teacher at Oracabessa Primary, Jamaica, guarded education with the utmost care. The desire to impart knowledge and prepare her students for the world seemed to burn like a flame within her breast. And she was determined to make us understand the value of an education in a country where only the privileged few got an opportunity to move onto higher education. In retrospect, Miss Parker exemplified the empowered spirit of Nanny of the Maroons. She did all she could to bring the community into the school via authentic experiences. Spelling bees, pageants, essay contests, sports day were all communal affairs and her students were the key players, with unencumbered space to demonstrate our abilities. It seemed that anyone, from the town's only physician to the market woman, would stop us at any given time while we were walking home from school to challenge us to an on-the-spot spelling test or quiz us to name the parishes of Jamaica, the names of the political leaders, or the location of rivers, for example. Miss Parker was instrumental in fostering in me an awareness of the power of education and community as well as an enduring love of learning. One of my strongest memories is the preparation for and participation in the national hero's pageant on the life and contribution of Paul Bogle, the event that sparked my interest in Nanny of the Maroons. Perhaps it was then that the seed was sown; this desire to continue the storytelling and etch our history into the annals of written literature to endure from generation to generation, pushing its way into the official discourse.

Oracabessa Primary School sits across the street from Oracabessa Wharf, now owned by Chris Blackwell and renamed James Bond Beach. Growing up in the seaside town of Oracabessa, my heart pulsed in rhythm with the excitement of my connection to Nanny of the Maroons, a Black woman of African heritage who lived and fought in my homeland, Jamaica. She planted seeds for me to reap and nourish my life. I felt joyous that a woman had the courage and the strength to consistently defy a mighty army to earn the metaphor of a thorn in their side. Her story opened up a world of possibilities for me; she presented the other side of the mirror of what it meant to be a woman, the otherness of the female who was the nurturing care-giver whose central role was to take care of the family at home. Within the context of the plantation hierarchy, as a Black woman, she would have been regulated to a nonhuman status. Within the context of freedom, she demonstrated her humanity and her ingenuity as a warrior and community leader. Multifaceted, this dynamic character was majestic, militant, and Black. A warrior in the field, she pushed the boundaries of the female stereotype to etch an identity of female empowerment disrupting oppression.

Challenging Empirical Data: African Diaspora Women and the Assertion of Agency

Nanny's agency is similar to that of historical women who asserted themselves and intentionally engaged in nontraditional roles within the societies wherever they were located. In acknowledging the privileging of the story of Nanny of the Maroons in this text, I must also acknowledge the heroism and agency of many other Black women of courage across the New World landscape who fought courageously against slavery and the injustice it wrought, though very little is written about them within textbooks and other forms of recorded literature. Less than 100 miles away from Jamaica, within the Spanish colony of Cuba, in 1843 the Lukimi/Yoruba freedom fighter Carlota, along with three male counterparts, organized an uprising on the Triunvirato plantation, which spread to include several others. Like Nanny, she is revered within anti-slavery folklore as a warrior and a martyr who died in 1844 fighting for an end to slavery. She is memorialized in Cuba as an agent of change and a precursor to the 1959 revolution. The storyline etching together the heroism of warriors such as Queen Nzinga of Angola (1581–1663), who courageously battled the Portuguese for decades, and Mary Prince, who exposed the horrors of the Caribbean slave trade in her book *The History of Mary Prince: A West Indian Slave* (1831), is an important thread that connects the diverse communities of African descendants across the globe. This is a storyline that tells the story of how disenfranchised people find opportunities for creative resistance in marginalized spaces.

It is important that steps be taken to use innovative sources, including oral history, to fill the gaps in the empirical data which do not acknowledge the significance of these women's contributions. As Terborg-Penn (1995) stated, finding paths for recreating women's views about their experiences is essential. In using the frame of the African Feminist theory, she emphasized the value of challenging the empirical data and revising the secondary sources in ways that highlight the agency asserted by Black women throughout the Diaspora. She shared that from her research she has discovered that throughout various regions of the African continent, common values in women's experiences provided a synthesis that can be used to establish a model to view women of the Diaspora. She has discerned that the very ideology asserted by Nanny of the Maroons is re-conceptualized by African-descended women who stand up with great resistance to social, economic, and political threats to their communities. "Among the unifying themes I identified were the leadership of older women, several of whom were revered because of their spiritual powers and contributions to community survival" (p.14), she stated, emphasizing that like Queen Ann Nzinga (Angola), Grandy Nanny (Jamaica), and Harriet "Moses" Tubman (United States), these women sustained the community.

The story of Nanny can be one important way for "reconstructing the history of black people and other women of colour, whether their lives are lived in the Caribbean or other areas of the diaspora" (Terborg-Penn, 1995, p. 17). My work as an educator is self-consciously infused with the agency to emphasize the need to alter historical epistemologies in presenting Nanny of the Maroons' contribution to political struggles in the Diaspora. This story is instructive in bringing the world to disenfranchised children, especially as it shows how an ordinary person can muster the courage and the tools to become a human being of heroic stature.

Interestingly, this history of the fighting spirit of Black women during colonial and post-colonial times is not referenced in the history books used in schools. There is nothing that speaks of the innovative ways in which they tackled the inequities they faced and the creative ways in which they prevailed as leading figures in sustaining their communities. Colonial discourse on slavery and post-colonial societies has traditionally been told through colonial diaries and travelogues of the 17th, 18th, and 19th centuries. One has to read between the lines of such documents to get at the truth, for it was not in the disposition of the enslaver to highlight the bravery or valor of their victims. Told from the perspective of the colonist, the plantation world of the slaves and their colonizers was one of European civility and African savagery. It is one that portrays the planters' stereotypical reflections of what they considered the slaves to be, typically speaking/writing from an assumption of superiority in a manner which missed the resistance stance of the slaves and the authority of their cultural practices. "Those written in the 18th and early 19th centuries were couched in the language of pro-slavery ideology and were aimed at impeding the emancipation struggles on both sides of the Atlantic," Stolzoff (2000, p. xiii) affirmed, reminding us of the need to re-problematize existing theory and critique the dominant system of knowledge. Stolzoff continued that most of these chroniclers were supporters of—or at least apologists for—slavery. They were usually unable to detect distinct cultural patterns in what they were watching, as their prejudice clouded their ability to notice anything more than "impromptu" activities born of the "caprice of the moment" (Stolzoff, 2000, p. 29). Blinded by their notion of their racial superiority, they missed the nuances of the cultural creativity, practiced skill, and artistic imagination of Africans enacted in the daily rituals of plantation life. These were the very sources that nourished and replenished the African's capacity to stand up and prevail.

"In refusing to let the slave masters dictate their every move, the slaves advanced their own cultural agenda and political autonomy, gaining a sense of freedom and spiritual transcendence" (Stolzoff, 2000, p. 30). Quoting James Scott (1990), Stolzoff (2000) noted that slaves practiced everyday forms of resistance such as mocking, ridiculing, and generally avoiding work. In particular, he emphasized, the dance was used as an oppositional practice and rallying point for forms of political resistance and outright rebellion.

Nanny's Spiritual Transcendence

From the wellspring of memory, I pull the legends of Nanny, an inspired warrior and reflective leader charged with the agency for freedom. Her community respected her military prowess as well as her spiritual leadership and healing abilities. She was highly regarded for her connection to the land, especially with the daily evidence of her skills in utilizing its resources to assist in the fight against the Imperialists. Her commitment to guerilla warriorship was so inspiring to her community members that it became part of the vernacular that she was even more man than her husband Adu (Campbell, 1988). Folklore speaks of the science as well as the spirituality of Nanny with stories of how she used the land as a tangible force in her fight against the British. These tales reveal a symbiotic relationship with the land which directed, guided, and protected her and her people. She used the ravines, caves, and rivers as tools of empowerment, cunningly harnessing these natural properties to nurture her people and support them in battle.

One tale has Nanny deploying the rising steam from the river to stop the British soldiers in their tracks as they sought to attack the guerilla warriors in the interior of the island. Seeing steam apparently rising from a pot with no fire under it, the soldiers were overcome with fear, being reminded of the lore that Nanny possessed powers of witchcraft (obeah). Even as I tackled the emotional aspect of learning about the slave trade, these stories excited and emboldened me, for Nanny represented a fighting spirit that inspired me in its declaration that justice was always attainable; albeit not without struggle. She declared to me that I could pursue alternative paths in my own life. I simply claimed her!

Reflective Conversations: Question! Reflect! Write!

1. What important information about history does the author convey in this chapter?
2. What opportunities are there in your life in school to use the knowledge that you have gained from reading this chapter?
3. The author states that Nanny of the Maroons has played a significant role in the shaping of her identity. Write a summary of the author's discussion of the ways in which this historical figure has influenced her life.

References

Campbell, Mavis. (1988). *The Maroons of Jamaica 1655–1796: A history of, resistance, collaboration and betrayal*. South Hadley, Mass.: Bergin and Garvey.

Robinson, C. (1993). *The iron thorn: The defeat of the British by the Jamaicans*. Kingston, Jamaica: LMH Publishing.

Rucker, W. (2015). *Gold coast diasporas: Identity, culture and power*. Bloomington, IN: Indiana University Press.

Sharpe, J. (2003). *The ghosts of slavery: A literary archeology of black women's lives*. Minneapolis, MN: University of Minnesota Press.

Shepherd, V., Bereton, B., & Bailey, B. (1995). *Engendering history: Caribbean women in historical perspective*. New York, NY: St. Martin's Press.

Simpson, P. (2014). New Year's Day speech. Retrieved from Jis.gov.jm

Stolzoff, N. (2000). *Wake the town and tell the people: Dancehall culture in Jamaica*. Durham, NC: Duke University Press.

Terborg-Penn, R. (1995). Through an African feminist theoretical lens: Viewing Caribbean women's history cross-culturally. In V. Shepherd, B. Brereton, & B. Bailey (Eds.), *Engendering history: Caribbean women in historical perspective*. New York, NY: St. Martin's Press.

· 2 ·

FOSTERING THE INDIGENOUS SPIRIT

When you follow the path of your mother, you learn to walk like her.

—Ashanti Proverb

Tek Yo Han Mek Fashion

Identity theorists note the value of role models from one's cultural back-ground. They state how important it is for young people to see heroes and heroines reflected in their own image. Such images become symbolic of the possibilities for children to attain highly. Nanny, in particular, stood large as a remarkable symbol of liberation rooted within a history of colonialization, power struggle, emancipation, and eventual independence. Her story has had a profound impact on my identity and the practice I have selected to pursue. It is a story that admits to the vagaries of life and the vulnerabilities that impact us. Yet it is a story about the human capacity to acknowledge one's frailty and, with dogged determination, gather the resources at hand and move on. From the bowels of our storytelling, my teachers and family inscribed in our consciousness the Jamaican saying, "Tek yo han mek fash-ion." Translated, this means use any available resources at hand and fashion something creative from the diverse possibilities that life presents to tackle the challenges that confront you. Implicit in this worldview is the notion that failure is not an option.

In my West Indian History class in Jamaica I learned that this was the prevailing sentiment that characterized the Jamaican spirit following Emancipation, where many ex-slaves, making the transition from slavery to freedom, avowed, "me no ka fe hire out meself again." They chose to struggle to etch out a path of independence after hundreds of years of servitude. In this way, the ex-slaves asserted their autonomy by declaring that they would engage in creative endeavors to utilize the resources at hand to make something worthwhile. This ideology is reflected in the stance and economic viability of Jamaica's Informal Commercial Importers (locally known as "higglers"), who became an active and prominent force from the 1990s to the 2000s, and the Dancehall Queens of the same time period. These women's endeavors within the international marketplace, traveling overseas to purchase goods and resell them at a profit, demonstrate their ingenuity within a capitalist marketplace that would erroneously label them as simple market women. They represent the fighting spirit of women of the Diaspora, using every opportunity to *tek dem han mek fashion* and situate themselves without apology within the economy as breadwinners for their families. Similarly, the Dancehall Queens of Jamaica have forcibly entered a male-dominated marketplace to assert themselves as both a creative bloc and viable income earners (Stolzoff, 2000). These African Caribbean women positioned themselves as strategists rather than victims, gathering the resources at hand into economic and social strengths. This is the very spirit of survival and perseverance that Nanny and other women of the African Diaspora exhibited centuries ago.

Shepherd, Brereton, and Bailey (1995) emphasized the pivotal role women played during and after slavery, navigating themselves within the capitalist plantation complex to acquire their own economic viability. My investigation of colonial documents reveals both the outright and subtle ways women pushed back against injustice and asserted themselves. Bell & Morrell (1968) commented on women in Whitehall, St. Elizabeth, during the Apprenticeship period (a set of years earmarked for the gradual transfer of slavery into freedom), "Women and young people being particular aggressors; loose themselves of their former restraints, they set their unruly tongues also at liberty" (p. 395). Shepherd, Brereton, and Bailey reminded us that women were indeed not peripheral during the colonial and post-colonial period. Ex-slaves' resistance strategies frustrated and threatened to defeat the objectives of the Apprenticeship period as was stated by W. Williams, Chairman-Resolutions of the Parish of Portland, Jamaica.

> These intentions, as declared in the preamble to their Bill, were to promote industry and secure the good conduct of the persons to be manumitted. But these persons, instead of pursuing industrious habits, are not performing even half a day's work, while they are demanding a rate of wages far too exorbitant for any proprietor to afford, and at the same time are refusing to pay a fair rent for their houses and grounds. (Bell & Morrell, 1968, p. 409).

Storytelling and the Forging of a Radical Caribbean Imaginary

Such symbolic language, tek yo han mek fashion, pulled from the archives of our ancestral wisdom and typified in the actions of our local heroes, was central to my upbringing. These cultural elements created a reservoir of social capital that belonged to all of us; my classmates in school and the children in my community. From this reservoir, we pulled and nourished ourselves and our developing identity. Nanny of the Maroons was an important symbol in the collage of stories that shaped my adolescence. It was impressed upon me that I was not a generic child or student; I was one with a specific heritage and culture that includes critical thinking strategies and highly acclaimed skills. This storytelling shaped a conscious awareness of the influence of colonialism and the possibilities of countering its effects extending to my position today that educators must confront and disrupt the official discourse through story-telling of Indigenous culture.

Defiance and Assertion

While these stories were not written into the textbooks we used in school during my childhood, my teachers assumed the role of revolutionaries utilizing age-old techniques of the oral tradition to pass these stories onto us, embedding them into our critical consciousness and bestowing unto us a sense of connection to a colorful past and a radical Caribbean imaginary. These stories journeyed with me throughout the ages as I came of age in the era of the Civil Rights Movement in the USA, the developing international Women's Rights

Movement, and the liberation of island colonies (which were soon pushed to face another Imperialist monolith, the debilitating impact of the International Monetary Fund). Nearby, the Cuban revolution had led to the establishment of a socialist state intent on upholding sovereignty for its people. As the young Fidel Castro declared to his people, "we are not going back to slavery" (Netflix documentary, 2002), the winds of change in Cuba fanned cool breezes within our island and sharpened our sensibility to the value of collective agency. Prime Minister Michael Manley embraced the tenets of socialism and ignited a mass movement in Jamaica with critical appeal to youth and adolescents who became intellectually and emotionally engaged with the notion of being my brother's/my sister's keeper. We were quickened to the idea that our lives mattered, that we had a right to our independence and ownership of our land and our cultural mores.

Adolescent Inquiring Minds: Building Critical Consciousness

In high school, we read *To Kill a Mockingbird* and Harper Lee visited our campus and shared an afternoon with us sixth formers. Across the campus we read Dr. Kings' *I Have a Dream* speech, Eric Cleavage's fiery speeches, and opined about Malcolm X. At home, my father played a vinyl record album of Dr. King's speech over and over again each evening after dinner. Our critical consciousness was fostered by these transnational linkages and cultural transmission; this reading and arguing and reflecting was grounded in the particularities of our everyday practice and became a way of life for us. As we embraced ideas from across the seas, we connected them to what we studied and engaged in discussions about race and ethnicity embodied in our lived experience. Although a small country with limited physical and financial resources, we were constantly regaled with the history of our cultural prowess, our intellectual capacity to outwit even the most formidable opponents, as Nanny had done. This perspective that there are multiple ways of viewing the world, that there are diverse forms of achieving, was formed during these years long ago and served as a buffer against the hegemonic definition of human accomplishment I would later encounter.

Our teachers guided us in applying strategies of critical analysis of the changes taking place in the world and their impact on my island home, Jamaica. My studies of West Indian history at Excelsior High School, Jamaica, strengthened the conceptualization of the world as a site of struggle. At the sixth form level, we journeyed into critical analysis of our history, the meaning and impact of colonization, and the forging of the New World and our place in it. It was here that I became entrenched in the history and legacy of colonization, and an assignment by my history teacher, Mr. Randle (who later founded Ian Randle Publishers), asking us to write a journal entry from the perspective of a slave, strengthened my interest—and resulted in an authentic narrative that propelled me into the immediacy of the slavery experience and the resistance movement to disrupt it. This discourse played a significant role in socially constructing my identity (Gee, 2002; Moya, 2001) to forge a sense of self located in a broader cultural community where the notion of personhood was strengthened. Researching and writing my narrative as a slave woman whose resistance resulted in her being stripped of her clothes and publicly flogged by her master sharpened my perspective on the cruel inhumanity of slavery and extended my interest in exploring inequity and the deprivation that it fostered. It was empowering to acknowledge that resistance was also a central part of the script of the colonial experience, and Nanny loomed large in my imagination as a force to be reckoned with.

From the late '60s through to the '70s when I entered the University of the West Indies, and later, the '80s, I also recognized the many parallels and shared discourse between Jamaican Blacks and African Americans. Descendants of the ignominious slave trade, we were a people struggling for our human dignity, enmeshed in a civil rights movement that had long been born from the resistance movement against slavery. At the University of the West Indies, I pursued studies in global literature, including American literature, West Indian literature, and African literature, which served to expand my critical consciousness and understanding of how we are all connected across the universe, and I was able to cement my connection to the continuing struggle of Black people in former colonies to lift themselves from the despair of racism and poverty.

The Invaluable Records of the Past: Developing a Critical Imagination

At the University of the West Indies, the discourse of freedom and independence gained urgency with the teachings of scholars such as Professor Rex Nettleford, Maureen Warner-Lewis, and Trevor Munroe, who directed us to be proactive, remaining habitually critical of the society. Professor Nettleford (1978) stated, "The nation's commitment to nurturing its national identity and protecting its national heritage must be reflected in the proper care and preservation of the invaluable records of the past" (p.119). It is important to note that for people of color with a history of colonization, their invaluable records were preserved in their memories and the stories they passed down through the oral traditions. Professor Nettleford, a leading public intellectual, was also the leader of the country's premier cultural organization, The National Dance Theatre Company of Jamaica. This organization collected data, including oral history, and interpreted it in the form of cultural dance performances which both radicalized theatre and asserted the historiography of the nation in a manner that spoke to the past history as well as the contemporary positioning of the country.

Through his work nationwide, Professor Nettleford emphasized the value of building up the nation's historical consciousness and the imperative of turning our gaze onto our cultural roots to tell the true story of our heritage and our history. He incorporated the radical teachings of Marcus Garvey, whose work centered the African continent as a repository of power for Black people all over the world to gather strength, whether through physical repatriation or the dissolving of mental slavery, later reinterpreted by Bob Marley through the poetics of reggae music. The ideological defiance of the Rastafarians, who preached about spiritual karma and the righteousness of a Black God who would stop at nothing to set his people free was incorporated into the artistic outpourings of Professor Nettleford and the National Dance Theatre Company of Jamaica. From the connecting narrative of these sources, I learned that the stories told by Whites were based on the racist ideology of their claimed supremacy and their deliberate lies about the inferiority or savagery of Blacks. Professor Nettleford's work directly addressed the inquiring mind of an adolescent like me: *Why are things the way they are?*

Global Connections: Intertextuality

Nettleford (1978) spoke of the value of one's concrete experiences within the mix of the forging of a national identity. "Yet, it is the nurturing of this self-confidence that is the greatest challenge and hope for the cultural process in praxis" (p. 146). As the years progressed, Nanny became a speaking document of the West Indian female persona, an allegory of what it means to be a Black female growing up in Jamaica, and later, a woman of color in the Americas. She is a lesson in perseverance—sticking to one's goals even when the odds might seem to be against you. Connecting this story to myself, to other texts I was studying, as well as to big issues taking place in neighboring countries and across the globe, Nanny's story became an allegory: The fighting spirit of disenfranchised people rising up against oppression. This history of subterfuge and subversive acts epitomizes the West Indian mindset of freedom of will and freedom of action; one that is claimed by people throughout the New World seeking self-determination and autonomy of purpose. Guerilla warrior, female leader, community mentor, history defines Nanny as a multifaceted individual whose multiple realities defied, and continue to defy, stereotyped notions of what women can accomplish. Her story of inspiration is symbolic of the strength and capacity of the human spirit to face the odds and succeed. A powerful symbol of anti-colonialism, then, as now, Nanny's story remains a central part of the mythology of the West Indian experience, a living example of one who countered what might have been the discontinuity of our history, one who stared down the social injustices of her time with fierce determination and keen militaristic ability to establish a cosmology of agency, a blueprint for action that still guides us today.

The Shaping of a Political Ideology: The Narrative of African-Caribbean People

At the University of the West Indies my schooling evolved as more than just book-learning and examinations, revealing how our life narratives add to the integrity of our socio-political history, making it experiential and inclusive. I brought with me to the lecture halls and tutorial sessions of the university my own situated knowledge, including stories from my grandmother's kitchen and the village community. I brought the powerful words and colorful metaphors from my mother and my aunties' cautionary adages and I brought with me the exuberant imaginings of a child inspired by tales of possibilities. My scholarship engendered a sensitivity to disparities that lead to inequities, emphasizing the role I must play in bringing Maroonage to the fore in critical awareness that resistance practices so vital to the history of our people are under-theorized in academia and ignored in textbooks, which fail to examine how exploitation has replaced or tried to eliminate local cultures in the New World. The Maroons of Jamaica have provided us and the world with a prototype of how a threatened people can fight back against predatory practices of *super powers*.

These tangible examples of the resilience of oppressed people—many of whom travel on their journey with the feeling of being abandoned and alienated—must be shared, as they hold the potential to reassure and uplift children in our classrooms and diverse people across the globe, emphasizing that Black lives matter! As my situated identity evolved, so too did my narrative style, inscribed with gestures, color, vocabulary, and movement reflecting my Afrocentric heritage. This journey was enhanced by the study of African American literature, where cross-cultural textual interactions revealed a shared legacy thematically, socially, and historically with the life and times of warriors such as Harriet Tubman, the Moses of her people, and Sojourner Truth, a striking model of antislavery heroism. As I acquired these stories, I realized how they were very much an extension of a powerful lineage of Afrocentric culture, an inquiry into a magnificent past that must become an essential part of formal education as much as it remains the language/embodiment of Black peoples' story in what has been termed the New World.

At a crucial time in my journey I was strengthened by this conceptual framework of Black female identity crafted during the colonial period. From leaders such as Nanny, Harriet, and Sojourner, I have learned of the meaning of sovereignty and the ability of a people to articulate their vision of the future and to take steps to actualize it. This lineage of freedom- fighters emphasizes for all of us the ability to control our destiny and make creative choices. These warrior women present us with a framework to shatter stereotypes and reject the moral codes and values of a Eurocentric version of history. *Resolute, committed, and agentive,* they give us the courage to move through our fears, not around them, and to stand up and claim our birthright as human beings to be the best that we can be. Their stories are evidence of what can occur with determination and resourcefulness.

Live Free or Die!

Harriet Tubman (born 1822) participated in the metaphorical Underground Railroad during the 1800s, an intricate inter-connection of antislavery activists strategically located at key points, who were working to guide slaves to freedom. She escaped from slavery in 1849, at age 27, and traveled from Maryland to Pennsylvania, where she joined the anti-slavery movement and made 17 missions back onto the southern plantations, freeing more than 300 slaves.

Her heroic actions were grounded in the philosophy, "live free or die" (Animated Hero Classics, 2016). In learning the story of Harriet Tubman, an important piece of spiritual wisdom stood out for me, the advice she received from an elder to follow the moss on the tree, for the moss always grows on the north side of the tree. "If the moon don't shine, follow the moss," the story goes, emphasizing the value of the power of words and the spiritual reliance on the support of the land in the oral tradition of people of color in much the same way it did for Nanny and the Maroons of Jamaica.

Speaking Truth to Power

I have borne thirteen chilern and seen 'em mos' all sold off to slavery, and when I cried out with my mother's grief, none but Jesus heard me! And ar'n't I a woman?
—Sojourner Truth

Sojourner Truth, one of the most eloquent orators and anti-slavery activists, chose the name Sojourner Truth after having a vision that revealed she was destined to travel and tell the truth. The words, "Ain't I a woman?" so famously uttered by Sojourner at the 1851 Ohio Women's Rights Convention have earned her a place in both the historiography of slavery and women's rights. Having suffered the trauma of slavery and losing her children to its ravishing tentacles, she traveled the country preaching an eloquent message of racial and gender equity. She spoke forcefully and wrote passionately and went on to publish her memoir in 1850. What a magnificent achievement in a time of racial oppression and gender inequity! Sojourner also met with President Lincoln in 1864 and held conversations with him in which she agitated for Black people to attain their own freedom. Today, the US capitol houses a statue of her.

The agency of these revolutionary women not only repudiates the fallacy of the acceptance of servitude, it also reflects the strength of the historical continuity of resistance throughout the ages. The efficacy of the Maroons as freedom fighters was directly connected to this global movement of resistance and assertion of a Black identity. This anti-colonialist worldview evolved over time and continued throughout the ages to shape and influence movements such as Revivalism, Garvey's Negro Improvement Association, and the Rastafarian religion, the first of its kind in the Western world to acknowledge the presence of a Black God.

A Forced Migration

During the 1930s, Norman Manley and his cousin Alexander Bustamante emerged as leaders of the masses in the developing country of Jamaica. They soon split off into the establishment of the People's National Party (PNP) and the Jamaica Labor Party (JLP) and remain today the competing and leading two-party system of government based on violent rivalry. During the socialist era of the Michael Manley government in the '70s, my historical conscious-ness was strengthened by the focus on building a national identity and the institution of programs to improve the conditions of the masses. The PNP's implementation of what was termed free education opened the door for me to enter the University of the West Indies, paying nominal fees and supported by a student loan. This and other programs soon came under threat as the international finance community, under the leadership of the United States, took action against Manley's socialist economic programs and his diplomatic ties to Fidel Castro. Consequently, Jamaica was almost frozen out of foreign investment and loans as a result of US- led directives to the World Bank and the International Monetary Fund. Evidence also suggests that the CIA, working with the opposition JLP, undertook a clandestine program of destabi-lizing the PNP government in the name of anti-communism (Stolzoff, 2000, p. 101). This political rivalry engendered during the decolonization years has grown into radicalized enmity and the party loyalist, which has developed into an institutionalized system of violence. It is this very system, the political violence between the People's National Party and the Jamaica Labor Party, which pushed me to leave my country in the late '80s.

In the United States I found a system which continued the perpetuation of devaluing the rights of people of color and the heritage they carried with them along the circuitous routes of the Middle Passage into the Americas. Working in an inner-city school, I experienced the continued oppression of Black people, where children from low socio-economic backgrounds were labeled as failures and subjected to a regimented curriculum led externally by the local school district. From this location, labeled as an F school, I strug-gled to discern ways to encourage a sense of agency. I questioned myself and engaged in a personal/professional audit. This reflection initiated tentative steps towards the journey of social justice leadership and viewing the world through multicultural lenses. I asked myself, *what resources/skills do you have to embark on this journey?*

The Middle Passage and the Historical Continuity of Black People

As I struggled to navigate through the doubt and uneasiness, I reached the conclusion that it is important that our youth are exposed to the rich legacy of Black people; that they understand the heroism which has nurtured their existence and survival and that the adults must take the time to share these stories and provide them with literacy skills to promote their academic achievement. And so I turned to the historical and cultural knowledge of my ancestry as the foundation to move on. And while I did not yet have the critical consciousness or political agency that I do today, I committed to investigating the root causes of poverty and racial injustice in the classroom, which led me to the path of social justice and equity. I turned to veteran teachers at the school to seek their input and advice. I researched available community resources and made efforts to establish alliances that would bolster my ability to serve the needs of the students.

I found that individual and collective inquiry is an essential move towards seeking and developing equitable literacy classrooms. It facilitates questioning of school texts and seeks to find and share other forms and tools of analysis, and this often promotes a stance of resistance advocacy. I had begun a discourse which pointed me to the possibilities of bringing in other texts as critical ways of subverting the curriculum to include children's funds of knowledge and my own cultural storylines, including the stories of Jamaica's heroine Nanny of the Maroons and Haiti's Toussaint L'Ouverture, who, some sixty years after the Maroons' historic peace treaty in Jamaica, successfully led the Haitian Revolution, the first free Black state in the hemisphere. Although students of Haitian heritage comprised the largest sector of the school's demographics, this material had not been shared with them before.

Au (2011) stated that teachers' exploration of their own cultural identities must be the starting point in the quest to prepare them to teach effectively in classrooms with students of diverse cultural and linguistic backgrounds. It is this very perspective that strengthened my commitment to evaluate myself and investigate the value of culture in education. As someone who knows firsthand the struggles of disenfranchised people, I tell my story again and again. I recognize that it relates not only to a long-ago era, or to people of Jamaican heritage, but also to the current journey I am engaged in with the youth and adults that I serve in the USA. As essential as these stories were at the time of origin, they remain invaluable to communities today, for communities of all types and in all periods have used this mode, and the stories in themselves work to build communities. They transmit more than the plot or story; the telling of the story and the way it is told also becomes part of the tradition, developing legacy and the impetus for change. Like Sharpe (2003), I question the invisibility of Nanny in the canon and embrace Bilby's (2005) assertion of the empowering impact their cultural retentions had on the Maroons' achievements as Indigenous warriors who carved a place of belonging, both physical and psychological, within the Caribbean mindset. Mintz and Price (1992) cited Kamu Brathwaite,

> the Middle Passage was not as is popularly assumed, simply a traumatic destructive experience, separating Blacks from Africa, disconnecting their sense of history and tradition, but a pathway or channel between this tradition and what is evolved, on new soil, in the Caribbean. (p. xi)

The anti-slavery narrative of Maroon agency resonates as strongly today as it did centuries ago when Nanny cast aside servitude to assume the mantle of warrior woman to undertake guerilla tactics and fight against the inhumanity of slavery. It is a story that roots me to my heritage and helps me to convey to my students both the practical and symbolic effects of this woman who Sharpe (2003) called the most rebellious of the Maroons. This philosophical perspective of resistance and agency has been the foundation on which I constructed the world and remains the lens through which I view life. Funds of Knowledge Theory supports the perspective that stories bring communities of teachers, children, languages, symbols, and ideology together. These stories carried over the seas, in the dark, putrid hulls of the slave ships, nourished the people during the Middle Passage, and are the roots that hold us firm from one generation to the next.

The value of oral history is by now a well-documented educational praxis within Indigenous communities. Storytelling about the past in order to pass down history and wisdom to youth is an intergenerational practice used by the elders to teach about the world today. In order to contribute to the global social movement to democratize history, the voices of Indigenous people must be heard and must be moved from the margins of the historical discourse. We are now accountable to engage in ancestral writing as pedagogy that will bring hope to countless of disenfranchised people across the globe. Digital technology offers a set of innovative tools to record these stories and disseminate them throughout the world so that they accurately articulate the truth of our history. I stress how important it is to share these stories with all students, regardless of race or ethnicity, for we all have much to learn from each other. What we are paying attention to here is the fact that the records of people of African ancestry, and of Indigenous people worldwide, remain marginalized in textual records. As Toni Morrison urged, I have committed myself to write this book, the story of Nanny of the Maroons, to address this omission, even as I acknowledge that historically, all women have been denied their rightful place within the texts of Western civilization; that I am writing a book that I have wanted to read because I believe that this is a story worth telling.

Reflective Conversations: Question! Reflect! Write!

1. What evidence does the author provide to support the claim that women from the African Diaspora have demonstrated their commitment to survive and thrive?
2. The author states that political polarization pushed her to leave her homeland, Jamaica. *What factors motivated you to leave your homeland and settle here?* Ask this question of a family member, neighbor, or community member and share their response with your peers.
3. To what extent do you agree with the author that *this is a story worth telling?*

References

Animated Hero Classics. Harriet Tubman: Leader of the Underground Railroad. www.youtube.com/watch?V=gojj7DUYe58. Retrieved January 9, 2016.

Au, W. (2011). *Critical curriculum studies: Critical consciousness and the politics of knowing.* New York, NY: Routledge.

Bell, K.N. & Morrell, W.P. (1968). Select documents on British colonial policy 1830–1860. Oxford: Clarendon Press.

Bilby, K. (2005). *True born Maroons.* Orlando, FL: University Press of Florida.

Gee, J. P. (2002). A sociocultural perspective on early literacy development. In S. Neuman & D. Dickinson (Eds.), *Handbook of early literacy research* (pp. 30–353). New York, NY: Guilford.

Mintz, S., & Price, R. (1992). *The birth of African-American culture: An anthropological perspective.* Boston, MA: Beacon Press.

Moya, P. (2001). *Learning from experience: Minority identities, multicultural struggles.* Berkeley and Los Angeles, CA: University of California Press.

Netflix Documentary (2002). *Fidel*.

Nettleford, R. (1978). *Caribbean cultural identity: The case of Jamaica*. Kingston, Jamaica: The Institute of Jamaica.

Sharpe, J. (2003). *The Ghosts of slavery: A literary archeology of black women's lives*. Minneapolis, MN: University of Minnesota Press.

Shepherd, V., Brereton, B., & Bailey, B. (1995). *Engendering history: Caribbean women in historical perspective*. New York, NY: St. Martin's Press.

Stolzoff, N. (2000). *Wake the town and tell the people: Dancehall culture in Jamaica*. Durham, NC: Duke University Press.

· 3 ·

GAZING INWARD

The Efficacy of Communal Research

The doom of slavery is certain. I therefore, leave off where I began, with hope.
—Frederick Douglass

A lifelong journey of questioning and reflection grounded in the search for justice and equity, especially on behalf of children, led me to the Maroon Village in Charles Town, Portland, Jamaica, in June 2014. I attended the Charles Town Maroon Festival in a spirit of reflexivity, anxious to engage in an auto-ethnographic study to shed light on what has been a life-long pre-occupation with the Maroons. I found powerful expressions of affirmation that bolstered my commitment to promote cross-cultural dialogue as a methodology to break through imposed cultural barriers across geographical lines and became immediately attuned to an appreciation for the power of global diversity. The conference and celebrations opened up space for critical insight with an expansive view of Indigeneity across international terrain. What defined our community was the common experience of Imperialism and its enduring impact on us and our people. We identified the residual effect of intergenerational trauma. We examined the continuity of oppression of Black people in America, the dislocation of Aboriginal people from their land in Australia, and the denial of the existence of Native tribes such as the Tainos across the

Americas. There, a group of 15 researchers from across the globe, including those from Canada, Suriname, Dominica, Jamaica, and the African continent presented at the 6th Annual Maroon Conference on Indigeneity. The papers were presented by individuals all connected to the concept of Maroonage and Indigeneity, speaking on behalf of their ancestors and descendants who occupied fragile positions in a world they openly acknowledged as often hostile to their existence. While the atmosphere was emotionally charged, it also offered reassurance that Indigenous people were firmly rooted in the communities they occupied and that they were pursuing a body of scholarship that addressed the misconceptions about their background and current locations in the 21st century.

"When we start talking to each other, we know how we are connected. What we are meant to do," Dr. Marcus Waters of Griffith University emphasized in one of our discussions. "We must keep the fire burning by going back into the past to retrieve the tools to fix our future. We must reinvent who we are to connect to our present." The atmosphere was charged with the sense of community-building we experienced as Indigenous people forging an alliance with each other (Semali & Kincheloe, 2002) to support our work. We openly acknowledged the significance of this coming together as a route to breaking through the isolation and discouragement we often experienced. We agreed to pursue collaborative inquiry to explore our subjectivities as Indigenous people, support each other in our journey, and share stories of survival and triumph within the academic and broader community as important steps in building a body of work on Indigeneity as well as affirming maintenance of our cultural memory so vital to our survival and the survival of Indigenous people.

We are the Survivors
—Bob Marley

We acknowledged that trans-generational trauma continues to exact a heavy weight on our communities, exacerbated by acts of post-(neo)colonialism within the 21st century. And we acknowledged the value and dignity of each other's experiences, recognizing that within this sphere of our local contexts there was a particular uniqueness to the texture of the experience that strengthened the fabric of the global discourse. Scholar Erica Neeganagwedgin from the Center for World Indigenous Knowledge and Research, Athabasca University, delivered a poignant assertion of her people's legacy, noting that there are current texts that claim that her ancestors, the Tainos

(Arawaks), were wiped out. "We are here," she proclaimed, the presence of her mother and children in the audience a striking validation of her outcry.

Dr. Marcus Waters shared the dislocation of Aboriginal Australians from their ancestral land and the trauma this imposed on his people. He spoke of the rising suicide rates among pre-teens and teens crippled by despair before they had an opportunity to develop their talents and look to the future. Dr. Ann Bouie, an independent researcher from Washington, DC, noted the trend to remove the arts from schools, depleting cultural resources that were necessary to replenish the spirit of disengaged youth in the school system. I shared statistics on the performance of children of color in the school system of the United States, emphasizing ways in which standardization eclipsed the success of children of Indigenous heritage in schools, labeling them as failures. We shared these concerns so dear to our hearts, setting forth our ideology that our cultural heritage needed space to be represented in such a manner that our children could experience it, live it, and thrive from it.

For Waters, the story of Aboriginal warrior Dundalli is a counter-hegemonic force in the broader narrative of the survival and perseverance of his people. He spoke of ways in which the socio-historical culture of Jamaica had migrated to Aboriginal Australia and how the music of Bob Marley had touched the lives of his people. He shared the poignant story of how his Aboriginal mother had named him Marcus with the fervent hope that his life would be touched by the spirit of Jamaican national hero Marcus Garvey, a hope she fanned well into the future, even when her child was removed from her, a statistic of the Stolen Generation. This same hope, this same sense of optimism expressed by the group, was carried in the strains of Dr. Bouie's story where she emphasized the historical resistance and resilience of Black people during and after slavery. She shared stories culled from her research about the overt and covert forms of resistance that Black people were engaged in as they sought to subvert the deleterious effects of slavery. As these scholars shared their lives, their stories, and their scholarship, my own story rose up to find a place of belonging within this extensive global narrative of survival of our Indigeneity. I offered the story of Nanny of the Maroons as exemplar of the fighting spirit of Indigenous people who refused to succumb to servitude, who, through the genius of their creativity, countered the decimation of their physical body and managed to erect monuments of their cultural heritage that, though intangible in many respects, have continued to buoy up generation after generation in spite of new forms of oppression.

Reading Life Narratives: The Methodology
of Indigenous Research

In asserting this perspective of Indigeneity, we acknowledged the significance of qualitative methodologies in how we conducted research and how this research has much to do with how we experience the landscape today, and the ties to our ancestors and how they experienced the land in the pre-Columbian era as well as the eras of colonization and post-colonization. Here we were on Maroon land, engaged in a discourse that emphasized the value of research that involves self-observation, intercultural communication, and investigation agency within the special context of our history and our lived experiences, knowing full well that within the standardized world of academia we would have to push to assert this perspective on what counts as research. Our participation in rituals through food, drink, reflections and chanting, and music fortified us spiritually and engaged us in a lived experience of what it means to be a Maroon in contemporary times.

> Then she felt the magic, the African mystery
> —*The People Could Fly*, Virginia Hamilton

As I walked the earth of the Maroon village I felt a tactile connection to centuries of tradition. A connection which helped me to quiet the voice that tells me I have to be realistic when I want to be idealistic, for the Maroon village reminded me that a world of justice is possible; a fact that was discernible in observing the results of their intellectual, spiritual, and ideological resistance. Embraced within this cultural space, I welcomed the self-reflection, and the words and ideas expressed by my colleagues pushed me to probe and consider the question: *What matters most to you?*

Rising up from our conversations were many metaphors that pointed to the possibilities of answering this question. These were metaphors that reminded us of our place in life; how our multiple identities interact and fashion us as unique and complex individuals. Standing on Maroon land became a metaphor for our connection to our ancient roots. The food we ate symbolized the nourishment of our soul and spirit, while the participation in rituals and performance engaged us physically and metaphysically in the ancient lineage of our Indigeneity. The journey that led us here became symbolic of a stepping-stone towards pushing for that shift we advocated within the legal, educational, and penal systems. Yes, we affirmed: Through assertion of our storytelling we are making a conscious effort to change the conditions that seek to silence and marginalize (McLaughlin & Tierney, 1993, p. 5). We discussed how tapping into the symbolic power of cultural stories facilitated our decolonized approach to research and was one that required great effort to affirm and maintain within the scholarship where the very academic institutions we were affiliated with demanded empirical facts and methodologies that often discounted the efficacy of our Indigenous knowledge and what we knew to be our truth. This, we agreed, required us to stand firm as intellectual warriors of resistance. This experience emboldened me to seek the tools to continue the journey as a spiritual educational leader.

Might the Maroons of Jamaica present an answer to Eurocentric constructions carried over as inter-generational trauma that has mauled our children across the globe? I wondered as we spoke well into the night. I posed this question to my colleagues and argued with them about ways in which we too must act on behalf of justice and peace in the face of our parallel experiences and our interests in geography, displacement, and social justice and equity. We examined the history and effects of the Haitian Revolution, rebellions in Jamaica, and the attempts to eradicate the Native American tribes in the Americas, and realized the profound impact of Africa on the socio-cultural fabric of the Americas and new world communities in which we live. Our story straddles countries and histories and peoples to speak through the lens of anti-colonialism to emphasize the indomitable will of a people who refuse to be wiped out, as some sources have claimed; a determined people who refuse to be silenced.

One of the most remarkable benefits of this collaboration has been the realization of the potential of alternative, contested, or shared vision of our enhanced survival, well-being, and ongoing negotiations of identity. When we examine the deep crisis that has been there for years we become attuned to the necessity of engendering an understanding of the importance of working and advocating for a worldview and systemic change even while we address our particular local issues. While maintaining the collaboration we had initiated would be challenging, we agreed with Joseph Bruner that *the most subversive thing you can do is to show that something is possible.* Our experience in marginalization and injustice puts us in a unique position to investigate how to reform education for the better (Mohanty, 1997). Our approach validates the history of our people and serves to elevate the stories within the context of K–20 curriculum and within the community, countering the enormous waste that society inflicts on children when it denies them acceptance of their cultural background and their funds of knowledge as valid classroom material

(Yosso, 2005). This worldview grounded us in the quest to achieve social justice and equity, acknowledging that each of us has within us an extraordinary capacity to become an inspiring leader for healing, evolving, and liberating the world. We agreed that through our work we would explore the importance of articulating those values explicitly in social justice and equity work and so raise public consciousness. It was clear that we would rely on technology to facilitate this collaboration in the creation, collection, and sharing of our life narratives so essential to our research process. This visit was a rite of passage connecting me to an Indigenous community without borders, reminding me that the educator who works to weave the threads of courage across the generations can have such an effect on the soul of her students (Kessler, 2000).

Understanding and Interrupting Neo-Colonialism in the Classroom

While this book is rooted in my personal experience it provides a framework to examine teaching to diversity and disrupting the persistent marginalization of specific communities. Tapping into the history of colonization, it questions how and why schools have been structured the way they are and how that structure supports the current economic system born out of capitalism and slavery. As I will discuss in Part II, I have worked with students to explore how our stories are entangled across the globe and to show how themes are explored and connected among traditional texts and cultural stories that social-justice scholars are inviting into classroom pedagogy. It is my goal to train teachers in utilizing an experiential approach that incorporates auto-ethnographic frameworks to assess their capacity to meet the needs of children in their charge. This includes investigating strategies that may lead to actions that will improve teaching and learning at the school site. Teachers will understand the value of alternative data that is unique to their context, including students' multiple ways of knowing, and the cultural heritage of their communities. This includes identifying symbols of achievement within one's culture so that role models are specific and drawn from the child's cultural legacy. On this mission, I am faced with the question: *How can I recast my individual story into a group story in such a manner to share with my students, build their confidence, and inspire academic development?* In Part II I will present a practical example of the transformative classroom pedagogy that honors the cultural legacy of the community.

Reflective Conversations: Question! Reflect! Write!

1. Research rites of passage in Maroon culture. Create a bulletin board that shows various Maroon traditions/rituals in words and pictures.
2. What role has oral history played in the life of the writer of this text? According to the author, how has oral history worked to convey a particular perspective or point of view about Nanny of the Maroons?
3. Interview an older person in your family or community. Ask him or her to tell you about a person who has influenced or shaped their life. Record the interview with a question and answer format, then paraphrase and write a summary of the interview.

References

Kessler, R. (2000). *The soul of education. Helping students find connection, compassion, and character at school.* Alexandria, VA: ASCD.

McLaughlin, D., & Tierney, W. G. (1993). *Naming silenced lives: Personal narratives & the process of educational change.* London, England; New York, NY: Routledge.

Mohanty-S. (1997). Literacy theory and claims of history: Postmodernism, objectivity, multicultural politics. Ithaca, NY: Cornell University Press.

Semali, L. M., & Kincheloe, J. (Eds.). (2002). *What is Indigenous knowledge? Voices from the academy.* New York, NY: Routledge.

Yosso, T. J. (2005). Whose culture has capital? A critical race theory discussion of community cultural wealth. *Race, Ethnicity and Education, 8,* 69–91.

PART II
READING THE CURRICULUM
THROUGH GLOBAL INQUIRY

PREAMBLE TO PART II:
READING THE CURRICULUM
THROUGH GLOBAL INQUIRY

Send My Roots Rain

As long as there has been slavery in the New World, there has been Maroon presence enacting agitation and resistance, which resulted in the weakening of the tightly constructed institution of slavery. The Maroons' ability to resist and thrive was buoyed by their strong bond with their cultural heritage and the leadership of Queen Nanny. According to Sharpe (2003), "Maroons' histories of the war of 1734–39 center on the powerful nature of Nanny's science, and all of the stories of her powers are testimony to the Maroons' own cunning and bravery that won their freedom" (p. 7). The Jamaican Information Service (JIS) (2014) described Queen Nanny as "a Chieftainess or wise woman who passed down legends and encouraged the continuation of customs, music, and songs that had come with the people from Africa, and which instilled in them confidence and pride."

Maroon lineage has long been established as a large cultural frame that embraces belonging and identity for Jamaicans. The impact of Queen Nanny's pivotal force in the preservation of African culture and knowledge within Jamaican culture is accepted across the communities and she is highly esteemed as a leader who united the Maroons of Jamaica and established them

as a political force. After escaping the plantation system, Nanny utilized guerilla tactics to weaken the British stronghold. She and her brothers established a community of warriors within the interior of Jamaica, resulting in a
system that successfully freed slaves from the plantations while they damaged
plantations, weakening the economic stronghold of sugar production. The
Maroons proved to the planters that the demand for freedom was not an idle
threat as they continued relentlessly for over 150 years to remain a major
player in the circumstances that led to the ending of slavery. Their ideology of
resistance sustained the movement towards emancipation and eventual independence, and it is one that remains today, a spiritual and cultural identity
marker embedded within the ideological mindset of the Jamaican people.

The 21st-century Maroons of Jamaica have remained an intact socio-
political force. They have successfully stayed outside of the imposition of
Western politics and cultural domination to maintain their African heritage.
Known for their economic, social, and cultural development, the Maroons
are an autonomous community within the broader community of Jamaica.
They have maintained their political structure, governance, and social organization. From the very start they established themselves as a community of
practice based on the ideals of freedom. The heroism of Nanny and her brothers has established them as folk heroes within the recorded history of Jamaica
as well as its folklore. Nanny, in particular, is known for her leadership of the
Windward Maroons, while Captain Cudjoe of the Leeward Maroons is well
respected for his unwavering stance against slavery, which resulted in several
rebellions for which his notoriety spread across the nation to earn him folk
hero status.

The portrait of the heroism of the Maroons of Jamaica is useful as a
symbolic representation of how life, despite its many challenges, presents
us with opportunities to move ahead. This story can be embedded within a
constructivist inquiry stance to share cultural narratives with children as an
important step towards legitimating the cultural capital of Indigenous people,
providing a structured approach to bring together Western curriculum with
the body of Indigenous knowledge that remains a central force in Indigenous
cultures worldwide. This stance connects to students' funds of knowledge
by inviting them to share their heritage and present to the world characters in which they see themselves. Because of the pivotal role my schooling
has played in shaping my research in social justice, I anchor my work with
children on the belief that schools must create spaces for the encouragement
of critical thought where young people are provided with a number of ways

of interpreting the world and translating their vision into radical action. In pursuing this social-justice agenda with my students, I hope to ignite their intellectual curiosity about the folklore of Jamaica as well as encourage them to seek further information about the African Diaspora with such vigor as to radicalize their school community in the historical consciousness that Indigenous people have heroes too.

> Schools act as powerful agents in the economic and cultural reproduction of class relations in a stratified society like our own.
>
> —Michael Apple, 1990

The conceptualization of Indigenous people's resistance, resilience, and courage is significant as I adapt curriculum material and pedagogy to push for the historical awareness of my students. This presents me with the challenge to create equitable, inclusive, and communal space within our specific context and utilize texts as a window into the identities and experiences of my students. Concepts of self and identity are at the heart of my teaching approach. In particular, I rely on storytelling to help me understand the complexities of my students' lives and their family backgrounds and also locate my own storylines within that space. Such storytelling draws on a broad range of human activity that addresses issues of goal-setting, creativity, and perseverance. It is particularly important in the classroom because of its orality and the tools of performance and dialogue that it incorporates. Storytelling can be a healing force that helps to settle emotional chaos as well as work as a route to creative expression. It creates the space for collaborative work between student and teacher with the potential to evolve into a force to disrupt the institutional neglect and lack of concern for the cultural needs of children of African heritage.

Scholars have noted the healing capacity of storytelling and the potential it holds for guiding youth towards new directions in life. Within this genre, youth are often presented with characters who are challenged by the caprices of life yet are able to remain on their journey by harnessing resources that foster the strength that leads to their success. This is a powerful ideology that scholars such as Estes (1992) noted provides a powerful source of direction toward self-determination for disenfranchised children dealing with the complexities of their realities, including alienation, violence, and drugs. Storytelling is particularly engaging in the classroom because of its reflective stance as well as those kinesthetic elements of the performative domain which tend to capture students' attention.

For to be free is not merely to cast off one's chains but to live in such a way that respects and enhances the freedom of others.

—Nelson Mandela

This is the message that springs from the crucible of Nanny of the Maroons' story. It is the message I discerned while on Maroon land and it is the consensus I arrived at with my colleagues that I engage with in collaborative inquiry. It is one that resonates as strongly today as it did centuries ago when Nanny cast aside servitude to assume the mantle of warrior woman to undertake guerilla tactics and fight against the inhumanity of slavery. hooks (1994) spoke of the value of teachers forging close relationships with students by personalizing the curriculum and sharing their lives with them. As I reflected on the narrative possibilities of my own educational journey in relation to that of my students, I sought to theorize my personal experiences and relocate these experiences within the broader context of the social and historical development of the Black Diaspora and then connect these to the context of our classroom discourse.

This has led to a cross-cultural, intergenerational dialogue as we have collaborated in enacting curriculum as lived experience beyond the scripted norm. My work in education is buoyed by the philosophy of intergenerational teaching and lifelong learning, and it is clear to me that I have much to learn from the ensuing interaction with my students. This literacy engages us in a cultural citizenship that speaks to the possibilities for change. I therefore seize every opportunity to:

1. Teach within the seams by connecting personal and cultural stories to existing canonical texts.
2. Expand assigned texts into building global awareness, concentrating on what the textbooks leave out, and extend those storylines of what it means to be human to include the socio-cultural heritage of people connected to the African Diaspora.
3. Examine global issues of social injustice and inequity.

Exploring the empowering effects of Nanny's work serves to strengthen my capacity as a social-justice educator as I engage with my students in critical conversations about curriculum pedagogy and anti-oppressive/social-justice education. This helps to put issues of culture and history in the struggle for education and self-determination at the forefront of our agenda. So I paint this warrior of justice on my classroom mural as an example of an Indigenous warrior who countered oppression with creativity. I pull lines from my conceptual poem, Nanny of the Maroons:

> *Black woman free!*
> *She snatched freedom to her bosom & claimed it for me!*

I share these lines to emphasize how this warrior for justice has been a model of empowerment for me in the hope that my students will also make a personal connection to this story. I tell them that Nanny's story speaks to the will of any disenfranchised people who are determined to confront adversity and assert their rights. It also reminds those who hold power to answer to the call for human rights and justice.

Digital Technology: Extending the Discourse Across the Globe

This generation of learners has witnessed the movement from traditional print texts to include digital, visual, and performance pedagogy. I have worked to include these forms of critical pedagogy within my classrooms to inspire students to write, interpret, and create our worlds together. Through digital technology they are able to connect with other youths across the world, share their stories, and inquire into what's going on as well as respond to these developments. This enables them to tap into their political historical knowledge, placing them at the center of their educational journey, where they become expert knowledge producers and activists (Saavedra, 2011). Through each narrative we share, the rich texture of our community evolves to validate our efficacy as change agents.

In co-mingling my cultural storylines with those of my students, I am guided by Freire's philosophy (Freire, 1970; Freire & Macedo, 1987) of reading the word and the world with children. Freire (1970) stated that freedom is the indispensable condition of the quest for human completion, and I believe that storytelling must be an indelible part of this quest. For it is a necessary tool in the preservation of Indigenous knowledge production and a necessary weapon against attempted erasure. I am therefore intentional in establishing a praxis of informed action within the classroom where students are visible, their voices are sonorous, and together we are able to form a coalition of pedagogical action based on our shared sense of purpose. This stance eschews the banking approach so prevalent in Western education and elevates the voices of students within the classroom, acknowledging the cultural capital they bring with them. It is this very cultural synthesis that Freire espoused that I want to create in my classroom through a conscientization of the curriculum that rises above standardization to create a cultural space that pays homage to the cultural diversity that inscribes our educational system.

Working within this transitional era, I have discovered the critical role that images play in how children see the world and position their place in it. Intertextuality and the connections among and between texts shape who we are as learners and teachers. This provides an opportunity for educators to embrace a critical perspective and allow students to include visual material and cultural artifacts as classroom texts. In opening up to multiple literacies, including digital literacies and students' funds of knowledge, teachers are able to tap into an authentic curriculum to build students' academic capacity.

In the following chapters I will point to how educators can examine the emerging global realities of this neo-colonial era and pursue work that opens up space to seize the moment to work as interpreters of culture and curriculum (Kanu, 2006) as they tap into the redemptive possibilities of social-justice education.

References

Estes, C. P. (1992). *Women who run with the wolves: Myths & legends of the wild woman archetype.* New York, NY: Ballantine Books.

Freire, P. (1970/2007). *Pedagogy of the oppressed.* New York, NY: Continuum.

Freire, P., & Macedo, D. (1987). *The politics of education: Culture, power and liberation.* South Hadley, MA: Bergin & Garvey.

hooks, b. (1994). *Teaching to transgress: Education as the practice of freedom.* New York, NY: Routledge.

Jamaica Information Service. (2014). Retrieved from https://jis.gov.jm/information/heroes/nanny-of-the-maroons/

Kanu, Y. (2006). *Curriculum as cultural practice.* Toronto, Canada: University of Toronto Press.

Saavedra, M. (2011). Language and literacy in the borderlands: Acting upon the world through testimonies. *Language Arts, 88*(4), 261–269.

Sharpe, J. (2003). *The ghosts of slavery: A literary archeology of black women's lives.* Minneapolis, MN: University of Minnesota Press.

· 4 ·

NARRATIVES FROM THE CLASSROOM

Let a second generation full of courage issue forth; let a people loving freedom come to growth.

—Margaret Walker

McLaren (2015) stated that:

We desperately need a cadre of teachers to speak out and to create spaces where their students can assume roles as razor-tongued public instigators for the public good (p. 4).

My life story provides me with good reason to believe that storytelling will encourage teachers to seek out, identify, and seize opportunities to creatively support and engage children in deep and meaningful literary analysis, including the life texts they bring to the classroom which may serve as counter narratives to the traditional literature. Such appropriation will contribute to the shaping of these students into razor-tongued public instigators for the public good, as it should raise their historical awareness, facilitating their assertion of narratives that counter the monolithic texts of the Eurocentric paradigm. This assertion lies at the core of my ideology and commitment to support educational discourse and agentive action that elevates a communal consciousness where all people are afforded equality and dignity to claim their cultural identity. In the middle school classrooms where I teach Critical Thinking, I search for tools that will allow us to examine global issues of social justice and inequity and to consider how our experiences are not separate but part of the circle of the human experience in which we are all entangled. Freire (1970) pointed out that an important part of social justice work is to assert counter narratives so that people will know that there are other stories to tell and that these stories matter.

Utilizing metaphor as a key pedagogical tool, I model for students the process of storytelling using Nanny of the Maroons as a blueprint for agency. I seek to present a vibrant and relevant display of my cultural knowledge to connect to their own situated knowledge. I want them to see the content of their classrooms as more than just reading and writing; rather, as a way to critique the world, identify why and how they should take action in this complex world, and recognize in a deep and meaningful way the value of their cultural identity.

Painting a Mural of Possibilities

In those first weeks of school where we introduce ourselves and begin the tentative steps to get to know each other, I share my background as a Jamaican child and talk about the central role Nanny of the Maroons plays in my life. Knowing full well that I will be coming back to that again and again, I throw this story out with my students like a huge mural that creates a backdrop on our classroom wall throughout the ensuing months. On this mural we will locate our family narratives within a historical context. We will also paint together stories of local, national, and global dialogue about the struggle for human rights and what it means to be empowered. With this goal in mind, I begin to share my work and perspective on Maroonage through imaginative and non-fiction texts I have in progress. Through the lens of critical race theory, I engage my students in an analysis of the social, racial, and cultural aspects of the literature as I endeavor to complicate the texts we have been assigned as well as those I will add (McLaren, 1995). We will work collaboratively to build a classroom based on cultural relevance to foster our development of critical cultural consciousness as a move towards translating state standards and grade level expectations into practical and critical learning experiences.

I hold myself accountable to engage with my students in an investigation of anti-Black racism that has spanned centuries and continues today as global racism and injustice against Blacks based on the perspective of White supremacy. The savage inequities expounded by Kozol (1991; 2012) become central to our investigation of education across the ages, and we delve into the Civil Rights Movement and the significant role African American children played in the passing of the Civil Rights Act, 1963. Extending the curriculum into contemporary developments, we utilize news media, the Internet, and personal knowledge and experiences to investigate state violence, police brutality in local communities, and the systemic maintenance of racism within schools and the penal system. We extend this to examine the forms of resistance that marginalized people have enacted and the ways in which they rely on their heritage to empower and sustain themselves.

Nanny's story not only points to the racist ideology that was developed in the 16th century to perpetuate the myth of the inferiority of Blacks in order to justify the exploitation of their humanity in the form of slavery, it also offers concrete and spiritual possibilities of resistance. The actions of the Maroons and their achievements provide hope in the possibilities of agentive action to address the growing movement of mass incarceration of Black people across the globe: African Americans in the US, the Aboriginals of Australia, and other people of color in every corner of the 21st-century African Diaspora. It encourages us to pursue strategies to face the socio-economic exploitation that leads to financial degradation and the persistence of poverty and underachievement.

As a social-justice educator whose practice is enmeshed in the artistry of storytelling, I hold steadfast to the significance of the imaginative in building students' historical consciousness. Within the tradition of the Caribbean literary imaginary rooted in the philosophy *tek yo han mek fashion* (see chapter two), I create both imaginative and informative texts about Nanny of the Maroons and share the ideology that we are intimately connected culturally, socially, and politically. From the corners of my imagination I etch the story of Nanny onto the mural of our classroom discourse:

> The rope tightens around her neck threatening to choke the very life breath from her body. Her eyes close and the slave ship rocks. The movement jostles her back to the present and resolve rises up from within the deep recesses of her womb. She feels the tingling of her hands tightly chained to another and sweat from her brows falls gently on the cuffs that have entwined them. She reminds herself to keep breathing. Breathe and dream of land. For the memory of the land and her people brings her hope.

Over the next weeks, as our discussions develop and we engage in conversation about our heritage, I take the opportunity to share my background and convey to my students the cultural significance of Nanny of the Maroons, my heroine. I tell them that she came to Jamaica aboard a slave ship around 1685; her captors intended to push her into a life of servitude. I tell them that Nanny looked to the mountains and set her sights there. She escaped and set about stirring up trouble for the colonizers.

> She stands still...breathless, the leaves of the Kindah tree enshrouding her body, embracing her form as one with them. Her bare feet are firmly rooted in the soft red dirt, right hand tightly grasping the machete. The Redcoat approaches and she raises her hand ready to strike.

I tell them how the British hunted her; they called her obeah woman, old hag, and sought to undermine her. I tell them that feminist freedom fighter Nanny battled and beguiled the British until her courageous death in the 1750s. I tell them that as a member of the Ashanti tribe of West Africa, she understood the complexity of the land and its central role in the lives of her people. She embraced the Earth, welcoming its resources as part of her intuitive leadership and military strategy.

> She sits under the Kindah tree staring out above the mountain range, breathing in the magnificent beauty of the land. Her gaze follows the clouds drifting across the evening sky and a soft moan escapes her body. She begins to chant; the sound rumbling from within and she rocks with the movement, to and fro, calling on the ancestors for guidance for at the break of dawn she must be ready to lead her people in what she knows to be a necessary bloodshed.

I tell them that Nanny was known as the most rebellious of the Maroons. And I am deliberate in establishing the warrior/protagonist archetype wrestling with the forces of antagonism represented by the Imperialists. Revered as Queen Nanny, she used the guerilla tactics she learned in her native Ghana to confront and disrupt slavery in 18th-century Jamaica. She established a Maroon community that challenged the institution of slavery and helped to bring it to its ignoble end. The British were so challenged by the fortitude of this Ashanti warrior and her four brothers that they offered a peace treaty in 1739. Nanny disagreed with the ideology of the treaty, considering its implications for the resistance movement, yet she acted in solidarity with her brothers in the negotiated ownership of land and rights which remain sovereign to this day.

This story, carried over the ages, strengthens the roots of Indigenous heritage within the New World. Like many other stories shared across the globe, it is a monument to our people's indomitable will to face oppression and thrive. It stands in defiance of the Eurocentric notion that Black slaves settled into servitude and lived at the mercy or benevolence of the White man. By exploring stories of historical empowerment of people of color and centering on the different ways in which oppressed people resisted and continue to resist, I hope to emphasize the creative thrust towards community-building and affirmation of identity and ignite my students' interest in the lived experiences of others. I share with them the journey which has brought me to their classroom as both teacher and student, in anticipation that the storytelling will engage them in a sense of wonder as they experience the richness of cultural heritage as pedagogy. I center my work on the belief in the urgency to explore and expose the philosophy that underlies the Euro-centric curriculum that is taught in schools. In addition to the influence I want to exert with students in the classroom, I also want to make a contribution to the development of the curriculum on global competence so that not only will teachers benefit from the material, but they will also extend their knowledge, skills, and resources into their classrooms so that the effect is exponential. It is essential to engage in dialogue that acknowledges that we are not living in a post-racial society, as some would advocate. Race matters, and racism exists. We see this in the funding disparities between school districts, which lead to disparities between opportunities and chances of life success for some groups of students (Kozol, 2005). We see this in the institutional neglect and lack of concern for the cultural needs of children of African heritage in schools.

This speaks to the historical and specific construction of childhood and school experiences for some groups of children as a result of the unjust and cruel practice of elevating the lives of White students over those of children of color. In stories such as that of Queen Nanny, we embrace hope in knowing that we have the capacity to take action, and, as Gandhi stated, become the change we seek.

An activist pedagogue, I am also a dreamer; one who continues to look to the utopian possibilities of education; that there is indeed a better world for our children in the future and that it is in this moment that we must take action to make it happen. For Indigenous people it is always a double-edged sword; resisting oppression and domination while nurturing idealism and elevating our cultural heritage within the disparate locations in which we find ourselves. Within the radical Caribbean imaginary, I see Nanny's story as that of the heroine stepping out into the world on a mission that she feels charged to accomplish. Tapping into the literary tradition of the heroine's journey facilitates my move to position Nanny as one whose story can be a model of agentive action for youth to emulate. For indeed, she represents the human capacity to be vulnerable yet also resilient and accomplished. I believe that her story holds the blueprint for how to make this utopian wish of educational equity a reality.

Small in stature, yet mighty in courage, Nanny evolves from history as a guideline for social justice work. The impact of the socio-cultural position-ing of her legacy can strengthen the academic identity of children of color. It should help them to see how injustice is reflected in the discrimination that takes place at the systemic level and how that leaks into the day-to-day experiences that continue to curtail the life chances of groups of people. In addition, this storytelling is readily connected to testimonials from all cultures and walks of life, so that all children, regardless of racial or ethnic background, can see the value of this form of pedagogy as they see themselves rooted in it.

Contemporary Manifestations of Nanny: Thematic Connections

I hope that something of the storytelling, the myths, and the history we will peruse together will rise from the sea of narratives and hold true in their minds where they can imagine a world better than the one we occupy today. I tell my students this story because I hope that this will be an effective approach in building their historical consciousness. I want them to see how the story resonates across the ages to give meaning to our current realities. I hope that as I reveal my background and ideology through this assertion of resistance and empowerment, they too may find courage and purpose in the portrayal of this magnificent woman whose narrative should provoke their consideration of the central role of their culture, and their own role as caretakers of the past and agents of change.

In searching for opportunities to teach within the seams of state standards and the assigned curriculum, I connect historical, cultural, and personal sto-ries to existing canonical texts and ask myself the question:

> What steps can I take by way of an ideology or direction to engage my students in a pedagogy of courage that will raise their historical consciousness and embolden them to act as agents of change?

The question pushes me to focus on the social, historical, and political forces that shape race relations and people's location within the society and the community. The efforts and initiative of ordinary citizens become graphic illustrations of people resisting marginalization by utilizing the resources at hand to grasp the change they seek. The Women's March on Washington in defiance of President Trump's inauguration becomes a topic of discussion in January, 2017. As we view the movie, *Selma, Lord, Selma* we interrogate the role of Sheyann Webb as the youngest civil rights activist at the time. We pair this with Teaching Tolerance's *The Children's March* and engage in deep heartfelt discussions about the children of Birmingham whose persistent efforts gnawed at the cordons of the racist city of Birmingham until Bull Connor was removed from office and President Kennedy passed legislation which later was signed into law as the Civil Rights Act. We hold a Socratic Seminar on the Black Lives Matter movement and reflect on the murders of youth including Trayvon Martin and Michael Brown. The images of Trayvon and Michael, young Americans who died early as a result of violent racism in this country, rise up on our classroom mural as graphic imagery of the pervasive loss of Black youth cut down in their prime. And I introduce the work of my co-author, Marcus Waters, in Australia, sharing with them the profile of the youth group, Aboriginal Warriors of Resistance, which he mentors. These become striking examples of the agency of youth engaged in contemporary movements of change; ordinary people taking action. We encapsulate the immediacy of these living examples into the metaphor of hope, courage, and action we are inscribing into the discourse and painting on our classroom mural.

By personalizing Nanny's story with stories of courage and resistance from across the globe, I am harnessing the authority of history to bolster an ideology which I consider it my crucial responsibility to share in guiding my students to become razor-sharp critics (McLaren, 2015). This creates the space to explore oppression, not only in relationship to Africa and the USA but also in Australia, and to extend this to the rest of the world. In time, my students should be asking thought-provoking questions as they examine how the status quo has remained to assign power to particular groups while seeking to exclude others. My greatest hope is that they will also find the tools to tackle this injustice.

I am motivated by the notion that it is important to strengthen the association between classroom pedagogy and local and global developments in politics and culture (Spencer, Knobel, & Lankshear, 2013), as this form of pedagogy will disrupt the patriarchal unidirectional, linear method of teaching and create a linkage with the past and provide a route to better understand the conditions of our society today. The activism of scholars who work to foster students' global competence and connect them to the international community directly addresses my search and becomes the foundation on which I pursue my own interpretation of instructional activism. I am deeply influenced by bell hooks' (1994) assertion that teachers must attend to both the intellectual and spiritual development of the child, and Apple's (1990) view that autobiography is an essential part of the instructional process. Not only have I found solace and reassurance in Paulo Freire's work, but I have also bridged his intellectual fervor with that of the military dynamism of Queen Nanny to forge the guiding principle that the community must be a foundation of resistance and empowerment. I am buoyed by the realization that there are strategies to overcome the historical social barriers that weigh so heavily on my mind, for the classroom is a fertile ground to take action and initiate change.

Memories of my classroom experiences in Jamaica inscribe my journey, always reminding me of my personal accountability, and I embrace the articulations of resistance against disenfranchisement that abound within the African Diaspora of my Jamaican roots. I carry these cultural expressions with me as an affirmation of Blackness; a refusal to be dominated. Holding firmly the socio-political lenses through which I view the world, I am nourished by the historical consciousness of working-class people who, from the very beginning, established a historical record of challenging the status quo in the Jamaica of my childhood. These are ordinary people who defied Eurocentric elitism to speak Patois, the much-maligned language of the common man; create reggae music; elevate Dancehall rhythms; and fearlessly pronounce the righteousness of the Rastafari religion. And all this, fortified by the political autonomy of the Black man nourished by the legacy of his African heritage so eloquently pronounced by Marcus Garvey.

These movements, like Black Lives Matter today, reflect the continuum of a world in continuous development, and all fit well with the advocacy that Nanny's story represents; that idealistic yearning for a better and just world, including a transformation of the educational system. It teaches us that we need to strengthen environmental sustainability and communal living rather than push for individualism and capitalism. What a contrast the Maroon community provides to the Western obsession with accruing goods and being better than your neighbor! This is a story that provides us with ways to reflect on the strength and diversity of Black people around the globe as it creates an insight into the enduring struggles for justice throughout history. It emphasizes the struggles that are shared across the globe among people who have been traditionally marginalized. I believe it can be used as a tool to explore the historical roots and contemporary manifestations of social inequity and the resulting discrimination and yet uphold a message of hope.

How Are the Children?

How will social justice educators respond to the age-old African greeting: *How are the children?* What indeed, are we doing to address the racialization of childhood in history, educational research, and classroom practice? As the persistent achievement gap between White and Black students widens, we are all implicated in the racial events in various cities in the US and other parts of the world where youth continue to be marginalized. Addressing these questions at both the emotional and professional levels, my move then is to create a multiple resourced space that values the students' funds of knowledge and incorporates my background rooted in the context of this particular place and enmeshed in sound literacy practices. As my colleagues and I had acknowledged at the 6th Annual Maroon Conference, Asafu Yard, Jamaica 2014, teaching and learning within the context of the secondary classroom creates the opportunity for teachers to engage with students in authentic ways to translate conceptual global multicultural education into K–20 instructional strategies.

At the time, we argued that too often students think that the textbook is a fixed-value free system of knowledge. We reflected on the fact that our story and history is either excluded or marginalized in the textbooks and agreed that we needed to critique the system as well as propose a course of action that will mobilize ourselves, our peers, and our students for change. In particular, we needed to cultivate in students a critical and reflective disposition necessary to overturn the deficit approaches to the study of people of African descent in schools. With this line of inquiry, I hope to raise my students' intellectual consciousness that classroom texts are historically, socially, and ideologically constituted.

Students' Life Narratives: Why Is the World the Way It Is?

In this eighth-grade Critical Thinking classroom of 22 students from diverse racial and ethnic backgrounds we come together as a community of practice in August 2016, amidst the turmoil of the US presidential elections. And much like I did decades ago, these adolescents are eager to pursue the question, *why is the world the way it is?*

The school year opens up with an opportunity to bring the world into the classroom and raise the students' critical thinking and appreciation for diversity. Master Drummer Willie Stewart of Embrace Foundation, a former member of the renowned Third World Band from Jamaica, brings to our school the drums of the ancient world, sharing with the students a presentation marked with all the elements of an excellent instructional plan and the emotional pull of loved ones gathering in a spirit of celebration. He uses the sound of the drum to call us together, reminding us that across the continents we are one. One people united in a universe that embraces us all under the same sun; a universe that sings in harmony with enough resources to fulfill all of our needs. The rich verbal and kinesthetic aspects of the presentation engage my students' hearts and imagination, erasing the distance between student and teacher, child and adult, and the intensity of the experience is clear as they are enthralled by the presentation, asking questions, rocking to the beat of the instruments, dancing.

This audience of 200+ eighth-graders is enthralled in lessons on the history of drums harkening back to ancient times through to the development of the New World and today where drums continue to speak to a digitally connected world, uniting us in one common language. "This is the cell phone of ancient times," Stewart tells the students, referring to the talking drum. Their interest piqued, he engages their full attention and goes on to demonstrate how the drum was used to communicate across the land, informing people of breaking news such as impending wars, imminent weather, cries for help, as well as celebratory announcements such as births and baptisms. He has touched upon the very intersections of history and the Americas that is so central to my instructional thrust. And I am thrilled!

Mr. Stewart further explains how this drum mirrors the rhythmic tone of a human's voice with the ability to communicate with similar levels of emotions. He invites the students to touch and play several of the drums, adding a tactile, kinesthetic, and sensory element to the presentation, which delights the students. Utilizing dialogic literacy, he shares how drums continue to be central to cultures across the world, grounding the people in a sense of belonging. Students experiment with the Brazilian surdo, the agogô bells, and the Nyabinghi of Jamaica. They listen intently as he speaks of the healing effects of music and the fact that it works to connect us with the rhythmic flow of the universe, guiding us to a place where the rhythm speaks to us in a common voice very much like the rhythm of our heartbeats and our footsteps across the Earth. He strengthens this perspective by asserting that we all have an umbilical connection to the drum. Students are actively engaged in the presentation as Mr. Stewart guides them to interpret and present dances, respond to thought-provoking questions, and in the end they form an undulating conga line, sashaying across the room to the final rhythms of the drums just minutes before time is called and they are ushered back to the classroom.

Returning to the classroom, I capitalize on the opportunity to position the students' voices within the context of instruction as they deconstruct the meaning of this cultural experience. It is with great enthusiasm that the students engage in post reflection, excited to weigh in on their particular experience, as indicated below.

> Willie Stewart touched my heart with his music. He showed me how beautiful music can be and it can bring people together. Music makes you want to just dance and release stress and pain and relief will flood you. I feel happy and filled with relief. Music triggers your feelings and emotions. I loved how dedicated he is to his work and culture. He is proud of his job and his heritage. He is Jamaican. When everyone got up and danced I can't explain how happy I felt.
>
> —Adriel

This critical/reflective/probing space ignited by the presentation offers a third space for more in-depth exploration of global cultures and the factors that shape who we are today. An authentic learning experience such as this creates the space for children to speak back to the classroom pedagogy and bring their knowledge and experiences to bear on the school's literacy practices. It highlights how teachers may guide students to present their work to peers and critique each other's work—not just as consumers but as producers of texts and critics themselves. In this manner, they develop critical inquiry skills as they engage both non- traditional texts, including the stories I bring to them and those they bring as well—stories important to their everyday lives—and mix these with the canonical texts rooted in specific genres of literature that we are required to study.

I continue building on the discourse through utilization of diverse and critical texts as a framework to investigate themes of historical injustice and provoke my students' informed commentary on racism, identity, and equity. This is a crucial move, I believe, to disrupt the continuation of the racist legacy of classroom texts. My objective is to expand their perspective on the themes of exploration and discovery and push towards developing historical consciousness:

What tools can I use to push students to be skeptical of what they read, to ask questions and open the path to experience different points of view?

I center this essential question as a guiding force in developing the curriculum with my students. Tapping into the tenets of critical literacy, constructivist inquiry, and culturally relevant pedagogy, I succor intellectual stamina from critical theorists such as bell hooks, Bill Pinar, Prudence Carter, and Gloria Anzaldúa, questioning multiple perspectives, conscious of the extensive work and findings of how the curriculum used in schools reproduces structures of inequality and oppression. I give deep consideration to strategies to use provocative literature, films, visual and written media, including material from websites such as Teaching Tolerance (https://www.tolerance.org) and Facing History and Ourselves (https://www.facinghistory.org), as well as YouTube and History Channel videos. This material helps me to examine the past, revisit the national record on civil rights and racial matters, and encourage students to construct their own ideological viewpoint within the classroom based on their background juxtaposed alongside contemporary developments, pushing forth the perspective that fairness is a fundamental right and that people coming from different corners of the globe have different experiences and those experiences add value to the landscape of our classroom community.

Broadening and deepening our studies beyond the classroom with texts that present real- world examples of Indigenous warriors provides potential inroads for students to both value and learn from the inherent diversity of the culture within our midst and connect it to the history of the region. Incorporating social, emotional, political, and academic goals, I set out to investigate if educators such as me can enrich students' understanding of cultural values. As we examine the pervading impact of colonialism, can we move them much closer to altering their perspectives about the place of people of African heritage in the New World? Can we disrupt the seemingly enduring Eurocentric paradigm that devalues the contribution of Black people to the development of the society? The instructional calendar provides me with the canvas to pursue this form of critical pedagogy focusing on the idea that texts can be created by students themselves.

As the weeks develop, so does my confidence that the students in my classes will connect to my personalized rendition of Nanny of the Maroons, especially as I have made moves to position myself as a social justice educator by the multimodal texts I use in the classroom designed to instigate reflection, conversation, and social action. Further, I chair the school's multicultural club and have created a multicultural pavilion in the hallway documenting the contributions of diverse social and cultural groups, including themes such as Jewish heritage, Native American studies, African American heritage, Hispanic heritage, and international women's history. I intentionally seek to engage their interest by elevating contemporary music such as reggae from Jamaica, rap in the United States, and reggaetón in Latin America, as part of the curriculum, guiding them to investigate how these forms of music may be interpreted as articulating the social history of disenfranchised people.

Most of the students are familiar with Bob Marley's music and we listen to the lyrics of "One Love" and discuss how this works as a metaphor to emphasize our common humanity. The students respond with enthusiasm to the poetic devices and especially the use of metaphors carrying strong messages of hope and possibilities through agentive action. We discuss the view that when one nurtures hope and combines that hope with agency, there is the possibility to experience the world as a better, more humane site of being. Marley's songs help to expand the space for us to explore themes of hegemony, apartheid, and dispossession of Black people across the globe. Within the Caribbean Diaspora, Marley's music and the genre of reggae music act as alternatives of history texts, providing audiences with narratives of slavery, resistance, and emancipation; alternative realities that are ignored or historically downplayed in the literature and in education. It is music that occurs at the intersection of race and class; culture and history, and as such speaks to the very theories that are explored in this chapter. This music is important to me as an educator researcher of Caribbean heritage and a classroom teacher who utilizes music including music from the Diaspora as important elements of classroom pedagogy that incorporates alternative materials other that the generally accepted canons that emphasize a Eurocentric worldview.

The textbook we are assigned by the administration includes stories covering a few of these topics; however, they are not critical or political and tend to uphold the hegemonic definition of human accomplishment. And so we engage in collaborative inquiry, examining what stories mean in all cultures as we push the stories from the textbooks as an effective stepping stone to begin, stay committed and empowered to continue that journey. Aware of the themes they are also studying in social studies, I connect Nanny's story during the years of slavery in Jamaica to the Atlantic slave trade and the infamous Middle Passage and point out that since the journey of Africans on the Middle Passage to various locations in the Americas the people's survival has rested on the power of memory-keeping. Indigenous people have used language to evoke the memories and shared inheritance of their culture. These remembrances played a pivotal role in the survival of African ancestors during the horrendous 400 years of slavery. Today, these stories are vital to us, the memory-keepers, who have a special responsibility to continue to weave the patterns in the tapestry that tells of our struggle to carve out a destiny of independence. They are especially important in conveying the essential message of the heroism of Black people in the New World; highlighting the fact that we did not settle into and accept servitude, but like the hero/heroine from antiquity to contemporary times, we stepped out into the world to face our deepest fears, and in doing so attained monumental accomplishments. In examining the journey from the Middle Passage to slavery, emancipation, Jim Crow, and the Civil Rights Movement, I ask my students, has the dream of Dr. King been realized? One student's response in particular pushes me into a critical/reflective stance on the long and enduring struggles of the Civil Rights Movement:

> I do believe that we have fulfilled Dr. King's dream. Dr. Martin Luther King Jr.'s "I Have a Dream" speech was that for all men to be equal regardless of the color of their skin. Even though racism still exists today, we as a society have made enormous improvements. For instance, Black Americans are in every part of our government system, like the legislature, executive and judicial branches. We have had our first Black president elected in 2009–2017, which was Barack Obama. We also have Clarence Thomas as a Supreme Court justice. As you can see there are many famous Black people like Will Smith in "I am a Legend." 60 years ago in the South nobody believed they would ever have had a Black president. These are the reasons I believe we have achieved Dr. King's dream.
>
> —Justin D.

Reflective Conversations: Question! Reflect! Write!

1. Identify and discuss one strategy the author utilizes to build the historical consciousness of the students.
2. To what extent do you agree with the author that storytelling functions to keep people intimately connected culturally, socially, and politically across the globe?
3. What is the author's purpose in including the students' written commentaries?

References

Apple, M. (1990). *Ideology and curriculum* (2nd ed.). New York, NY: Routledge.

Freire, P. (1970/2007). *Pedagogy of the oppressed*. New York, NY: Continuum.

hooks, b. (1994). *Teaching to transgress: Education as the practice of freedom*. New York, NY: Routledge.

Kozol, J. (1991). *Savage inequalities: Children in America's schools*. New York, NY: Crown.

Kozol, J. (2005). *The shame of a nation: The restoration of apartheid schooling in America*. New York, NY: Crown.

Kozol, J. (2012). Fire in the ashes: 25 years among the poorest children in America. New York, NY: Broadway Books.

McLaren, P. (1995). *Critical pedagogy and predatory culture*. New York, NY: Routledge.

McLaren, P. (2015). *Pedagogy of insurrection: From resurrection to revolution*. New York, NY: Peter Lang.

Spencer, T., Knobel, M., & Lankshear, C. (2013). Researching young children's out-of-school literacy practices. In J. Larson & J. Spencer (Eds.), *The Sage handbook of early childhood literacy* (pp.133–160). Thousand Oaks, CA: Sage.

· 5 ·

CREATING CULTURAL SPACES
IN THE CLASSROOM

Culture is the widening of the mind and of the spirit.

—Jawaharlal Nehru

A reading of Diamondstone's (1999) "Tactics of Resistance in Student-Teacher Interaction" motivates me to expand the assigned texts into building global awareness and conscientization of the curriculum (Freire, 1970). The personal essay "Bonne Annee," by Jean-Pierre Benoit (2015) in the textbook, *Florida Collections Grade 8* (pp. 31–36), is identified as an anchor text and required reading by the school district. I reference the colonial origins of the Haitian people to establish the historical connection with the text. Bonne Annee tells the story of a young boy, born in Haiti and raised in the United States by parents who yearn for the removal of the dictator Papa Doc's regime from their beloved country so that they can return home one day. The story provides just the opportunity I desire to launch into a critical discussion about current immigration and inequity in the United States and to step backwards into the past through to the Haitian Revolution and the heroic achievements of Toussaint L'Ouverture, whom I recall from schooling in Jamaica as one of the most critical figures in the movement against slavery. My students have not heard of the name and so I share with them information regarding L'Ouverture's warriorship against slavery in Haiti, uniting the different groups of slaves and free people to rise up and defeat the French. I emphasize that his astute leadership fueled a revolution that led to the declaration of Haiti's independence in 1803. I also share that this revolution undermined the system of slavery throughout the hemisphere, and like the work of Queen Nanny, it conveyed the message that slaves could rebel against their masters, and this in fact helped to bring the institution to an end. Warriors such as L'Ouverture and Queen Nanny set the example of what the possibilities were. In addition, in strategizing to create a community of resistance, L'Ouverture called on enslaved people from other countries to come to Haiti and live and work. He supported Simon Bolivar and the freedom movement across Latin America. By challenging the world economic system of slavery, he set an example for all peoples who were suppressed.

In keeping with Pierre Labrosiere, I share with my students that the response of the imperialists was brutal. L'Ouverture was captured by Napoleon Bonaparte's army and died of pneumonia in a prison in France in 1803. Pierre Labrosiere of the Haiti Action Committee asserted that L'Ouverture's work had so challenged worldwide hegemony that Haiti became the place to be defeated (iam Cheyna, 2015). The world responded by isolating Haiti and made it pay for rising up against White supremacy and the hegemony of slavery. Incensed by this uprising against its political hegemony, France maintained the constant threat of invasion, with warships continuously circling the island, a graphic and intimidating gesture in the threat to invade Haiti and reoccupy it as a slave state. In keeping with the imperialist thrust of the era, France demanded reparation of the slave owners' property in compensation for all the profit from the slaves they "lost" as a consequence of the revolution. Labrosiere estimated that the fine imposed against Haiti would be equivalent to $21.7 billion today. He stated that Haiti was forced to shut down its schools in order to funnel these funds towards payment of this crushing debt. A consequence of this arrangement is the underdevelopment of a public school system. Latin American scholar Paul Burke (iam Cheyna, 2015) noted that at the time the USA was run by slave owners committed to the doctrine of slavery. He cited, for example, that Thomas Jefferson and George Washington were all slave owners, and Haiti's revolution threatened the very fabric of an institution from which they succored their legitimacy and supremacy. The US didn't recognize Haiti as an independent country until Abraham Lincoln did so during the Civil War, almost a half a century later. Haiti had its first free democratic elections in 1990.

That whip was a slice open cut of pain
—*The People Could Fly*, Virginia Hamilton

In assigning a review of this video, I am hoping to stir up my students' historical consciousness and enlighten them about the world conditions which shaped that country's origins, and which have resulted in a pervasive poverty that continues to characterize the economy and lifestyle of the Haitian people in contemporary times. I work to elevate this story, especially as two of my students are of Haitian heritage. However, they seem to have no awareness of this historical background to their heritage. I realize that I am entering delicate terrain considering both the stigma that has been traditionally connected to Haiti in our south Florida community as well as what I perceive might be emotional issues for these children.

From here I step back even further as to how slavery was started in the West Indies and how it established a particular order of existence. I am then able to connect Nanny of the Maroons to the resistance movement of Toussaint L'Ouverture, with the plan to move on to other selections in the textbook covering Frederick Douglass and Harriet Tubman in the months ahead. Although I consider the textbook material to be bland and uncritical, it nonetheless allows space to subvert the standardized curriculum and invoke a critical stance. We work in a whole group session to complete a concept map on slavery and explore ways in which the after-effects disrupt lives, feeding into the cycle of migration and dispossession today. I consider this to be a strong foundation on which to probe the historical and contemporary causes of poverty and inequitable standard of living for certain groups in the United States and the world.

A Socratic Seminar focusing on Christopher Columbus and his role in the development of slavery in the West Indies poses the question, *Should the US celebrate Columbus Day?* I am surprised that several of the students state that yes, he was deserving of such an honor. This makes me think about how we are influenced by how we see others and the world.

We should celebrate Columbus Day for without him we would never have found North America. He found America and later brought back goods to Spain. That is how we also found out that the earth was round. Since people went to live in America because of the riches, we became a nation even though he found it by accident.
—Anthony (Hispanic American student)

Yes, I believe we should celebrate Columbus Day because he was the one who found America and he spent months trying to find land and he did. His bravery really came upon his voyage going across harsh seas just to find land. This is a real important accomplishment to celebrate and acknowledge his great voyage. It wasn't easy going across those 100 foot waves with not the greatest ships. But he was determined and he did it. All America should remember his voyage and celebrate it!

—Luke (European American student)

I support celebrating Columbus Day because it represents the Age of Exploration and America wouldn't be what it is if it wasn't for Columbus. Yes, he did kick out the Indians, but his actions bridged the gap between the Old World and the New. I celebrate Columbus Day because that day should be recognized for the bravery of Christopher Columbus.

—Dante (Italian American)

While I recognize and accept that these students are entitled to their perspective, I also feel that their position might be uninformed, or that they are possibly feeding into, or accepting, a view perhaps expressed by their parents. Then, as now, I am faced with the challenge of how to transform mainstream curriculum into social justice text and work with students to develop positive and democratic attitudes towards diverse cultural, racial, and ethnic groups and to produce writing that reflects their developing historical consciousness. I realize the need to complicate what we have learned about the past and examine texts in school that present a racialized perspective about the life of Indigenous and colonized people. Such practices remind us of the urgent need to investigate and push back against policies that uphold a racialized system of power which allows for educational oppression and its continuation.

This brings me face to face with the realization that in this suburban community it is important to challenge students' internalized ideologies and subjective identities, especially in light of the district-assigned Eurocentric curriculum that typifies teaching and learning at the school. I decide to use questions and prompts over the weeks to guide them to explore these issues with the central question in mind:

How Do We Correct History?

I want to encourage my students to reflect and comment on important events in history and their lives. At the same time, I want to be careful not to privilege my interpretation over the meaning that the children arrive at as they strive for meaning-making in our classroom. How might I use storytelling to help students to embrace the concept of being culturally responsive and culturally sensitive? How might I use my cultural background, as well as my current work in social justice, as a resource for my students, who are, in essence, being prepared to become future leaders of our society? I interrogate myself as I reflect on J. F. King's (1991) push against dysconsciousness and the view that an uncritical habit of mind may uphold inequity and exploitation by accepting the order of things. This is perhaps one of the greatest challenges facing educators today; the necessity of having students understand how past realities have created current inequities and the significance of building their capacity to take agentive action within the classroom through discussions and sharing of perspectives.

The unfortunate facts are that the textbooks used in school focus on pedagogy that interprets history through the dominant national narrative, and that the activities engaging students remain Eurocentric and continue to imply, if not overtly state, that the Caribbean and African Diaspora ways of being in the world are somehow inferior to that of the Eurocentric way. It has been embedded in the textbooks, and thus within the consciousness of children, that explorers, Columbus chief among them, came upon primitive peoples who lacked the enlightenment and sophistication of the Western world. This over-simplified view of the European arriving bearing gifts and opening the eyes of the native to a more sophisticated life that he should be grateful for is one that is over-simplified, unquestioned, and often unchallenged in textbooks and classroom discourse. In keeping with McLaren (2015), it is the duty of the critical educator to devise strategies to challenge such a perspective and encourage children to participate in a community of global citizenship.

A unit on Native American heritage expands our scope to explore their magnificent contribution to the development of the United States in particular, and the world in general. Moving beyond what I see as a generic way of acknowledging their history, I push my students to consider the attempted genocide that had taken place, and we discuss the Native American philosophy that led them to share with the Pilgrims, a factor which led to the confiscation of their land and terrible battles and loss of life. As a follow-up, an excerpt from the book *Morning Girl* (Dorris, 1994/1999) works as an instructional tool to focus on adolescent identity and cultural heritage. Students connect to this story, where Taino Native, Morning Girl, lives on an island with her parents and younger brother in pre-Colombian times. When she questions her identity and physical features, her parents direct her to the beauty and grace of her physique, making connections to the natural landscape about her through metaphor, simile, and graphic imagery.

Recalling my colleague's commentary on the attempts to erase her Taino heritage from history, I capitalize on the students' interest and return to the story of Christopher Columbus. An Internet search provides an interesting article with a simple, but thought-provoking, question that grabs my attention and paves the way for the insightful analysis I crave which may help me to probe further without negating the children's perspective or silencing their voices.

> Who are the Tainos? The U.S. Government says they are extinct, but they are not. Most likely you might know them as Latinos, a Spanish speaking person of Latin American (the Spanish speaking part of the Americas, south of the U.S.) descent. Not all, but many modern day Tainos are unaware of their lineage. To understand how that could happen you must know the story from the beginning (The Tainos, 2016).

The article goes on to discuss that on the very first night, Columbus wrote in his journal that these islands were very heavily populated by a handsome, strong, well-built, and peaceful people who had only simple weapons and that with as few as 50 of his men and their weapons he could take over. I use this article as the basis for further interrogation of Columbus' impact on the development of the New World, the development of the slave trade, and the agonizing centuries of slavery, with its continuing aftermath to this day. Students work in small collaborative groups to interrogate the text and share their perspectives, building their historical awareness of this monumental time in world development. They continue to argue and disagree, however, what strikes me as most important is their critical awareness of the forces that converged to shape the Americas. And while this particular whip of history remains an open slice of pain for me, I also acknowledge that my role is that of facilitator of the discourse and I resist the urge to privilege my perspective over the dissenting voices, inspired by their growing historical consciousness.

Reflective Conversations: Question! Reflect! Write!

1. Why are the comparisons the author draws between L'Ouverture and Nanny of the Maroons important?
2. To what extent do you agree with the author that stories give meaning to our lives? What might be the essential meaning a student of Haitian heritage derives from the story of Toussaint L'Ouverture?
3. Based on the information presented in this chapter, what is your response to the question, should we celebrate Columbus Day?

References

Benoit, J.-P. (2012). Bonne annee. In *Florida collections Grade 8* (pp. 31–36). Orlando, FL: Houghton Mifflin Harcourt.

Diamondstone, J. V. (1999). Tactics of resistance in student-teacher interaction. *Linguistics & Education, 10*(1), 107–137.

Dorris, M. (1994/1999). *Morning girl.* New York, NY: Hyperion.

Freire, P. (1970/2007). *Pedagogy of the oppressed.* New York, NY: Continuum.

iam Cheyna. [Screen name]. (2011, July 24). *Haiti The untold story* [Video file]. Retrieved from https://www.youtube.com/watch?v=6nskDm2yhPA

King, J. (1991). Dysconsciousness racism: Ideology, identity, and the miseducation of teachers. *The Journal of Negro Education, 60*, 133–146.

McLaren, P. (2015). *Pedagogy of insurrection: From resurrection to revolution.* New York, NY: Peter Lang.

The Tainos. Retrieved from https://www.tumblr.com/search/native%20

· 6 ·

READING THE WORLD

A Praxis of Global Citizenship

In every generation action frees dreams

Wayne Au (2011) supported the idea that there is a strong link between compelling personal stories and the strategies for teaching. This link may generate spiritual artistic experience and intellectual insight, he asserted. Inspired by this perspective, I seek material that should connect to students' home culture and encourage them to examine how they negotiate their own identity in multiple spaces. The intention is to build empathy, respect, understanding, and connection as we share stories in the context of this cultural space we are co-creating.

I believe that such critical consciousness may guide students to discover ways to disrupt any borderlands that exist so that they may see the similarities between their unique and nuanced cultural practices and those of their peers as well as other people across the globe.

Cultural stories such as that of Nanny of the Maroons should help in the breaking down of fabricated differences and serve to establish a tolerant environment based on understanding, empathy, and compassion. It is here, I believe, that I see most clearly my purpose for teaching, as my objectives and strategies mesh with the students' vision and their presentations echo with the confidence of their interpretation and understanding of their cultural heritage.

What does it mean to be a cultural individual? How do you and your cultural heritage fit into the United States of America's national history? Is every culture worthwhile and valid, even though it may be quite different from what we experience here in the United States?

These questions elicit heated conversations, with students discussing diverse experiences they or family members went through. While most students share positive comments about celebration of their heritage, a few students speak of incidents where parents or grandparents experienced discomfiture in public places because of their limited English proficiency. In an interactive journaling between parents and the students, one student shares his mother's reflection on a time she experienced language discrimination and how it made her feel diminished at the time. The student reflects that a waiter had denigrated the status of their family members and the heritage of their language while they were dining in a local restaurant. Another taps into the historical background of his native Haiti as he regales us with stories about mealtime with his large, animated family. He explains that the food most highly prized by his family has its origins in cast-off items from the masters' kitchen that slaves made edible and enticing with the spices they used and the slow method of cooking. There is a gush of enthusiastic responses from students who share the value of family gathering and the role of food in their culture. It is clear these memories are arousing meaning that are central to their identity.

Testimonials of Cultural Legacy

You can hear the candle wicks burning on the menorah in my house during the winter holiday. I spend Hanukah with my marvelous family as we eat different foods. We eat foods called Kugel and what that is a baked pudding or casserole, most commonly made from egg noodles. We find this dish amazing because it is warm, delicious and savory. The sweet desert at the end of the nine days is something called hamantash. A hamantash is a filled pocket cookie or pastry. We use these foods to lighten up the holidays like a lantern and blanket in a dark and deserted room. The hamantash is a delightful and as sweet as cake on a bitter day, with its delicious butter cream frosting. These foods are so important to our culture because they bring our family together for a sweet savory treat. This means we unite together using our culture and also to show how much we love each other. It expresses it in a way of bringing multiple extraordinary foods of our culture while loving each other by remembering our history. Each family member brings a different dish. These foods have an amazing effect on my culture and our celebration together as a family.

—Avery (Jewish American student)

I walk down the stairs and I smell the delicious smell of arepas in the kitchen. My parents are both Venezuelan and they love making arepas. Arepas are like crispy corn pancakes. Arepas can be eaten with anything you want inside them. You can eat them any time of the day. The traditional arepa is eaten with eggs, butter and cheese. The best part of an arepa is when you break it in half and the gooey cheese falls down like a waterfall. The outside of the arepa is crisp but the inside is soft. Arepas can be spicy, plain or even sweet. Next time you go to a Venezuelan restaurant, order an arepa!

—Maria (Hispanic American student)

We are building cultural space together and the elevation of the students' voice within the curriculum strengthens my move to position culture as a living, vibrant, experience that not only speaks of our past but also who we are in the moment. Encouraged by this new opportunity to explore the importance of familial and communal relationships, I pose the questions: *How might a people write themselves into history? How can we begin this process in our cultural space?*

I am encouraged by the students' interest in making connections to their cultural history, examining their relationships with school, friends, and their navigation between worlds. I recognize that we are growing in our awareness of what it means to participate as a culturally responsible citizen in a globalized landscape. This extends the space for social, historical, and cultural elements to intersect in expression of the way students experience the world, and I am inspired to collaborate with three other educators and the students from the Multicultural Education Club to craft and host an International Heritage Day in honor of Black History Month. And here, the personal history of the school community comes rushing in with a critical intersection with the curriculum and pedagogy at the school.

Students, faculty, and administration respond to the call to make meaning for ourselves and also to present meaning to the audience and rest of the school community. The program focuses on three key areas; students performing elements of their cultural heritage through dance, song, poetry, and drama. The presentation includes an interpretive dance to Maya Angelou's *And Still I Rise*, and three male students, one a Jamaican, another Jewish, and the third Haitian, interpret and present King's *I Have a Dream* speech. A second focus is the Ethnic Dress Parade, where students present ethnic dresses representing the diversity of their heritage, including the Cuban guyeraba, the Nigerian agbada, the Spanish flamenco, and the quadrille dress of Jamaica. The school choir enacts renditions of songs from the Civil Rights Movement, and "This Little Light of Mine" ignites the room as the students evoke the imaginary of a gospel hall meeting.

This cultural space enacted by the students strengthens our efforts to build a community of practice as students perform and engage with texts of their own creation. In these presentations they portray the complexity and the humanity of our diversity as they create, share, and empower themselves as critically conscious cultural beings. Through this inquiry experience, I feel my own vision of social justice work is being nurtured by my students' journey. We are united, teacher and students, in creating a live text where we are able to explore the cultural diversity of our lives, interrogate stereotypes, and assert our cultural identity. Igniting their curiosity, encouraging their engagement in argument and debate, and fostering their drive to research and ask questions and complicate the status quo, now extend my vision.

Students Enacting Their Cultural Lives

We spend some time discussing and writing about this experience, examining footage of photos and videos captured by a team of their peers from across the grades. As we continue this exploration of the meaning of culture, I make a deliberate move to guide students to connect their cultural heritage to that of Indigenous people across the globe, such as the Maroons of Charles Town Jamaica, and delve into their funds of knowledge to create artifacts that honor their heritage. One morning, Mia brings in an egg box with half a dozen beautifully decorated egg shells filled with confetti, a visual display of a small but significant aspect of her cultural heritage. She shares the importance to her family of these cultural objects; hollowed-out eggs filled with confetti or small toys. At Easter, family members "smash" the eggs on each other's heads for fun and to wish them new birth and long life. According to Mia, "Now cascarones are a representation of the past and how we used to show appreciation of each other."

Using this visual display and Mia's cultural story as a point of interest, I guide my students to create cultural artifacts such as totems, dream catchers, and Stars of David, using these visuals as symbolic tools to make connections and strengthen the cultural studies we have undertaken. Shawna-Lee creates a totem of a butterfly on cardboard and she inscribes,

This symbolizes how I was at first. I was quiet and not focused. Now I spread my wings and express myself.

This cultural space that has evolved within our classroom has helped to establish a common ground for understanding and motivated the students and me to honor our cultural diversity even as we locate our unique attributes within that space. These first-person narratives created by my students give voice to their identity, expanding their worldview beyond the narrow confines of the mandated curriculum. My students are seeing themselves as cultural beings who might have different narratives from those in the texts and recognizing that other people do as well. This becomes a stepping stone to using this form of literacy as an opportunity or tool to construct relationships, share experiences, and create meaning among us. As our narratives evolve and connect with the texts we expand our classroom mural into a larger socio-cultural world and students begin to reshape their understanding of the world and their place in it. They draw from their lived experiences and knowledge to shape the texts they write, reading the world and offering up their perspectives (Freire & Macedo, 1987) and expanding their worldviews.

We exist in a complex web of lived experiences in relationship with our social worlds.
Is it repressive when important information about diverse cultures is left out of the curriculum?

I ask my students.

I share with them a video recording of Maroon children dancing at the 6th Annual Maroon Festival in Charles Town Jamaica, 2014. This helps me in concretizing Barbara Rogoff's notion of the cultural meanings given to events and the social and institutional support needed to uphold their meanings (Rogoff, 2003). In the video recording I made during my visit to the Charles Town Maroons, children aged 3 to adolescence are engaged in dancing the West African dinkimini to loud sonorous drum beats reverberating the ancient rhythms of Africa. The children's obvious delight in the movements of their bodies is a strong repudiation of any notion of inferiority or deficit culture. Here is a group of children whose moves were clearly not choreographed yet who are in sync with each other, jubilant and easy, a natural expression of their heritage and ongoing rituals. The children's autonomy and vibrancy display what has become a visual classroom text for me and confirms Lev Vygotsky's view that children in all communities are cultural participants. Through dance, rituals, and storytelling they demonstrate their agency as cultural transmitters. They project the efficacy of the historical child; one who is specific to time and place in history; not a generic student who must be standardized into formulaic education. This Indigenous practice so vital to their historical register tells us the importance of celebrations and intergenerational teaching. In this performance space, history is unfolding to tell a more accurate story of the lineage from the slave ship to the historical continuity of contemporary times. As I engage with my students in this text, I am engaging space within the seams. I use this video and the developing personal and historical consciousness about racial, cultural, and ethnic diversity to ground this concept within the concrete and material practice of my classroom and embed us in a chain of continuity that deeply stirs the soul of my students (Kessler, 2000, p. 27).

> *Who we are in relation to others? How is the dance of the Maroon children different from the dances that you do? How is it similar?*

Now several months into the curriculum, I feel that we are all better positioned to address the questions,

> *Whose voice should be heard? Whose perspective matters? How can we guide youth to develop agency and respond with creativity to the overt and insidious racism and discrimination meted out to others in the society or that they experience themselves?*

In keeping with my mission to incorporate authentic texts into the classroom pedagogy, I utilize an Aboriginal rites of passage text written by my colleague Dr. Marcus Waters, which my students read, review, and critically analyze in the classroom. They also review a video presentation by Marcus retrieved from the Internet and later participate in a live Skype session with him in which they take on the role of instructional leaders while I facilitate and observe.

As we share and deconstruct these texts, our discussions highlight the journey we have made in extending our perspectives to view the world through multiple lenses. We discuss how this story reinforces how rituals are cultural tools, the significance of these to both Maroon and Aboriginal cultures, to their understanding of identity and community. While the Maroons of Jamaica resisted and have maintained their sovereign rights to the land they earned as part of the peace treaties signed during the 18th century, Aboriginals in Australia continue under the siege of antagonistic policies based on the *Doctrine of Discovery*, which rob them of their birthright and access to their sacred land.

Aboriginal Australians: The Struggle for Autonomy

A shift into an interrogation of the ongoing forced removal of Aboriginal people from their homelands highlights the attempted denial of Aboriginality in their own country since the European invasion in 1770. Many Aboriginal groups in the remote areas, which Marcus calls Country, have remained virtually unchanged and resistant to European influence. Central to their way of life are spirituality, heritage, sense of belonging to the land, importance of family, and ancestry. Like the Maroons, the Aboriginals face inherent contradictions in maintaining cultural traditions, keeping the secrecy of tribal rituals and traditions from outsiders yet maintaining them and storing them for retrieval, especially in this digital age.

In its 2007 *Declaration of the Rights of Indigenous Peoples*, the United Nations criticized policies such as the Doctrine of Discovery as "racist, scientifically false, legally invalid, morally condemnable and socially unjust." The Doctrine of Discovery is still used to diminish validity and significance of international treaties between Aboriginal peoples and the USA, Canada, New Zealand, and Australia. Globally, such a perspective has been used to justify efforts to eliminate Aboriginal/Indigenous languages, practices, and world views and rob them of their sovereignty. Historically, this false presumption has prevailed, and remains deeply entrenched in the policies and culture of many colonial and neo-colonial societies, clearly demonstrating the hypocrisy of speaking of a post-colonial society (Waters, 2018).

Elements of the Doctrine have justified heinous behaviors against Aboriginal peoples through the centuries, with the Stolen Generations being among the most atrocious crimes committed against Indigenous children and their families. Between 1910 and the late 1970s about 100,000 Aboriginal children were abducted from their families. The government believed that Aboriginals had no future as a people and advised that their children should be fully integrated into White society and brought up according to White rules, customs, and traditions. The general aim was to assimilate or breed out the Aboriginal race. Many children were forced to grow up in orphanages or foster families, or were raised by White missionaries. Children were physically and sexually abused in addition to being used as unpaid labor (Waters, 2018).

Marcus emphasized that the ongoing forced removal of Aboriginal people from their homelands demonstrates the refusal to acknowledge their sovereignty as the First Nation people living in their own country at the time of European invasion. He noted that in Australia, Black people are under constant attack in the remote communities to which they have been relegated within a social and economic apartheid. While living in these third-world communities our water has been cut off and our homes destroyed in an attempt to once again forcibly relocate us to make way for mining. Our people continue to face violence as our past becomes embedded within the present. (Waters, 2018, p. 113)

Dispossession by propaganda, coercion, and blackmail is the term used by John Pilger (2015) to describe the Australian government's attempts to remove Aboriginal Australians from their homelands in order to excavate the land for mining and the wealth that comes with it. John Pilger, who has been investigating and chronicling the story of the Aboriginal in Australia since 1965, stated that the Australian government has embarked on a program to remove the Aboriginal from his ancestral land in order to accumulate wealth.

In response to Western Australia Premier Barnett's recommendation of the closure of over 150 remote communities, which would create over 20,000 traditional homeland refugees in their own country, Aboriginal Australia took militant action to disrupt this continued oppression and organized themselves into the SOS Blak Australia movement. In 2015 an estimated 25,000 people marched in a call to action around the country against the closure of their communities, with rallies taking place in Brisbane and Sydney (Wahlquist & Davidson, 2015; Waters, 2018, pp. 131–132).

Going as far back as the time of the British invasion, Aboriginals have had a long history of resistance and agency in fighting for the rights to their ancestral land. While the history of this resistance and assertion of their ancestral rights has been ignored within the Australian narrative of conquest and development, Aboriginal Australians continue to be inspired by stories of their historical agency such as the actions of Aboriginal elder William Cooper, who created in 1933 the first Aboriginal deputation to a commonwealth minister, seeking audience with King George IV during the king's visit to Australia. Although he was not granted an audience with the king, his petition was subsequently published in the *Melbourne Herald*, on September 5, 1935. His agency resulted in the celebration of the First Aborigines Day in 1938, which today is known as the National Aborigines Day and Islanders Observation (NAIDOC). Marcus and I carry the same concern about the exclusion of our Indigenous heritage from the curriculum in the schools that children of Indigenous heritage attend. For example, Aboriginal culture goes back 60,000 years, yet it has received very little attention nationally within the narratives of Australian history and literature. Australian textbooks and classroom lessons do not tell the truth that Aboriginal warriors developed highly organized guerrilla warfare against the brutality of the European invasion during the 1800s. There is no recognition of the frontier battles Aboriginals fought in Australian schools. The fact that for more than 60,000 years Aboriginals maintained one of the most sophisticated land-management systems in history is also missing from this narrative (Gilbert, 1977; 1988). Similarly, folklore such as that of Anansi the West African spider, which tells of the courage and perseverance of people of African ancestry, is missing from the literature of Western school books (Marshall, 2012).

I emphasize the symbolic essence of rites of passage, including the carving of totem trees, to establish Marcus's story as a point of reference to convey the notion that not unlike the Maroons, the Aboriginals demonstrate an enactment of strength through the occupying of communal spaces and the engagement in their cultural practices uprooting Terra Nullius. This story bears particular relevance to our line of inquiry as it conveys the reciprocity which enables the exchange of knowledge, for it is an autobiographical story deeply rooted in spirituality. As Marcus tells it, he demonstrates how verbal teachings are produced, passed on, and negotiated. He highlights for us how important it is to examine multiple ways of resisting efforts to silence his people. Engaging in this rite of passage with Aboriginal youth is one such method of resistance. Sharing it with scholars like myself is another. And working to get this story into publications is yet another step. Like the story of Queen Nanny, this tale fittingly emphasizes the power of Indigenous Knowledge Production as a tool that the Aboriginals of Australia have used to resist the push to silence them.

I share this story with my students from a funds of knowledge perspective, eager to have them make connections with their own history, culture, and heritage, and to stir up discussions about the connections of our common humanity. It is important that they see that this enduring philosophical and spiritual belief exists in real terms for real people. I want to impress upon them the value of my own work and journey in being able to connect with a First Nation individual across continents. Like my story of Nanny of the Maroons, Marcus' story becomes an important pedagogical tool. For while these stories might be considered marginal within Western academia, they are important to our experience, for such stories bring the past alive and reaffirm our place in history.

We extend this examination of the oppression of the Aboriginals of Australia to look at the resulting impact of such exploitation, as evidenced by the Long Grass Men; homeless Aboriginals who live in the wild, the long grass of the seascape their home. In researching the background of their story, the students gain new insights into how they became homeless Aboriginals; deprived of their rights to their ancestral land, their sacred property continues to be violated. As Marcus noted, this forced removal from the land poses a serious threat to the maintenance of Aboriginal culture, where the people are spiritually connected to the land. This destruction of culture erodes language heritage and negates the people's human rights and dignity. In the current state of 21st-century Australia, The *UN Declaration of the Rights of Indigenous Peoples* is ignored and their inalienable right to uphold their sacred relationship with the land trampled.

Reflective Conversations: Question! Reflect! Write!

1. To what extent do students' writing samples reflect the development of a cultural space within the classroom? What is one story you would like to share in your classroom?
2. According to the author, how can knowledge of the past shape the way we live our lives today?
3. Why do Aboriginal Australians continue to struggle for autonomy in their country?

References

Au, W. (2011). *Critical curriculum studies: Critical consciousness and the politics of knowing.* New York, NY: Routledge.

Freire, P. & Macedo, D. (1987). The politics of education: Culture, power & liberation. Westport, CT: Bergin & Garvey.

Gilbert, K. (1977). *Living Black: Blacks talk to Kevin Gilbert.* Ringwood, Australia: Penguin.

Gilbert, K. (Ed.). (1988). *Inside Black Australia: An anthology of Aboriginal poetry.* Ringwood, Australia: Penguin.

Kessler, R. (2000). The soul of education: Helping students find connection, compassion, and character at school. Alexandria, VA: ASCD.

Marshall, E. (2012). *Anansi's journey: A story of Jamaican cultural resistance.* Kingston, Jamaica: University Press of the West Indies.

Pilger, J. (2015, April 24). Evicting Indigenous Australians from their homeland is an act of war. *The Guardian.*

Rogoff, B. (2003). *The cultural nature of human development.* Oxford university press. Ebook. Retrieved October 2013.

United Nations declaration of the rights of indigenous people. (2007). https://www.un.org/development/desa/indigenouspeoples/declaration-on-the-rights-of-indigenous-peoples.html

Wahlquist, C., & Davidson, H. (2015, March 19). Close the Gap day: Colin Barnett tells protesters to "put yourselves in my shoes." *The Guardian*. Retrieved from www.theguardian.com/australia-news/2015/mar/19/close-the-gap-day-thousands-rally-threat-remote-indigenous-communities

Waters, M. (2018). *Indigenous knowledge production: Navigating humanity within a Western world.* London, England: Routledge.

· 7 ·

FROM THE FIELD TO THE CLASSROOM

Celebrating the Heroes of the Black Atlantic

My Words Will Never Die
—Paul Bogle, National Hero of Jamaica

Why is it that some groups are thriving while others are disenfranchised? How can an Indigenous group appropriate their culture and artifacts to assert their agency and attain social capital?

My engagement with these questions leads me to consider ways in which I can bring in global literature that expresses our common humanity and engage the curriculum in constant and fluid construction rather than a fixed pedagogical administration that excludes certain children. In exploring world literature with students I seek to convey the pluralism that defines America and the classroom, from the perspective of both student and teacher; insider and outsider. The storytelling genre provides a source of criticality which fosters the sense of conscientization that I am seeking for my students. To nurture the cultural consciousness that is already developing within the cultural space of our classroom, I turn to the rich possibilities of oral history to foster the development of a more socially conscious democratic society. The classroom textbook offers examples of folktales which provide the opportunity to share the richness of global culture and connect this to the students' stories from their family tapestry.

In our exploration, we have grown to recognize how each student's unique family contributes to a richer society as they become learning opportunities that help us to explore biases and prejudices and increase our understanding of our own multicultural selves. This engagement with multicultural literature and the stories from our homes increases the understanding of diversity and the cultural norms that shape us and the way we interact with the world.

I share with students Anansi stories of resistance and subterfuge from the West African folklore genre that is a fundamental part of my heritage, intersecting culture, geography, and values. We use these tales to interrogate how perspectives are crafted and conveyed. I share with them how in times of conflict and oppression, Anansi "has the potential to inspire a combination of psychological and practical methods of survival and resistance" (Marshall, 2012, p. 4). I share The Nine Yam Hills story from *The Confessions of Anansi* (Brailsford, 2003, pp. 73–77), which tells the story of Anansi's attempt to outwit Jamaica's national hero, Marcus Garvey. In this tale as is the case of the Anansi cultural legacy, Anansi is symbolic of the spirit of resistance and survival that slaves exhibited during the plantation era in such a manner that contributed to the dismantling of the system and the ending of slavery. "Anansi the spider-trickster of West African and Afro-Caribbean folklore was as significant a hero to the slaves as were the real-life heroes Cudjoe, Nanny, and Tacky" (Craton, 1982, p. 15).

Anansi is one of the most significant stories carried over by the Koromantees into the West Indies during colonization. Today it remains an indelible element of the consciousness of the Jamaican people, a testament to the counter-hegemonic discourse Blacks developed during colonization and sustained across the Black Atlantic throughout the centuries.

According to Marshall (2012), "Anansi has remained emblematic of Maroon and rebel resistance, as well as survival in modern Jamaica" (p. 114). To emphasize the continuing struggle and fight for freedom and elevate another hero from my culture, I then connect these folktales to the history of Paul Bogle, who fought for justice in post-emancipation Jamaica in 1865. I tell my students how freedom-fighter Paul Bogle used his platform as a Baptist deacon to galvanize the community, spreading his ideology of resistance and empowerment. In 1865 he organized the Morant Bay rebellion, calling for the end to the oppressive leadership that had persisted after Emancipation. Although Bogle was captured and hung, like Nanny he had stirred up the winds of resistance against hegemony, and ignited fires that would not be extinguished. Bogle became a folk hero during his time, and later, a national hero revered for his intuitive leadership and bravery. He is memorialized in poetry and folktales and songs as noted in the famous Third World song "1865 (96° in the Shade)," which presents the heroic Bogle telling the oppressive Governor Eyre, "My words will never die." Third World immortalized Bogle's confrontation with the Governor of Jamaica in 1865, making this allegory accessible to the Caribbean Diaspora in a format that is creative and inspiring. The lyrics of the song set to the inimitable reggae music highlight Bogle's courageous resistance even when faced with certain knowledge that he would die. The words, "today, I stand here a victim, but believe me, I will never die" speak to the indomitable will of the Jamaican people and people of the African Diaspora who have been victimized and disenfranchised by colonialism, yet compelled by their agency, resist and take action to confront and dismantle oppression. I recall how my teachers applied the use of imaginative language to give insights into ways in which the daily activities of our community of practice could be connected to the work of leaders such as Nanny and Bogle, asserting their story as guideposts for the journey we would undertake. I learnt from my early experiences the power of potential and the motivational impact of symbolic figures in the lives of children.

These stories resonate and remind educators like me that metaphor is a powerful tool in social justice education. There is compelling resonance in such stories, for they represent thousands of years of cultural history rooted in the timelessness of the Indigenous tradition. While these stories acknowledge the devastating effects of colonialism, they also highlight the creative thrust of Indigenous culture; a culture that provides the foundation which has facilitated the survival of a people over hundreds of years of struggle. The presence of diverse children in the classroom, including students of Jamaican, Puerto Rican, Haitian, African American, and Native American heritage in addition to Anglo American heritage enriches the space and bonds us as we explore the multiple interweaving links between people connected by virtue of experience with colonialism.

I draw their attention to the words of Dr. Martin Luther King as we engage in discussions about contemporary oppression and resistance:

> *Freedom is never voluntarily given by the oppressor, it must be demanded by the oppressed.*
> —Martin Luther King, Jr.

We draw parallels with Harriet Tubman and Sojourner Truth, feminist warriors of the American slavery landscape. My students investigate contemporary heroines of the modern era and their own time such as Anne Frank and

Malala Yousafzai. They investigate activist writers such as Claude McKay and Paul Laurence Dunbar and they embrace the affirmation in the words of Maya Angelou, *And Still I Rise*. They research First Lady Obama's work with children, fighting against childhood obesity, and celebrating poetry at the White House. They note that discrimination is still prevalent in the society and that they can work to empower themselves to become agents of change. They argue and challenge each other's perspectives and agree that there are heroes and heroines everywhere among us and concede that they too have heroic qualities. As the story of Black Lives Matter (BLM) evolves within the national landscape, we also begin the work of painting this narrative onto the classroom mural in line with our commitment to investigate social justice and equity. We examine how BLM began as a local outrage and developed to spark a national discourse and a global agency against the continued exploitation and the stripping of the humanity of Black people and other disenfranchised people.

A United and Pervasive Resistance

I should fight for liberty as long as my strength lasted, Harriet Tubman stated in the text we are reading from the Houghton Mifflin textbook. Intentional in choice of material following the guidelines of the prescribed text, throughout the coming months we continue our exploration of literature that enables us to engage in readings of excerpts of *The Underground Railroad*, the *Narrative of the Life of Frederick Douglass*, and *To Kill a Mockingbird*. We utilize visual multimodal texts along with the canonical texts and interweave students' subjectivities/identity. Extended writing assignments, including multiple paragraph essays and opinion pieces, enable students to substantiate their comments and responses with specific details from their texts posed against their own perspectives. This is innovative education which, I believe, is preparing them for multiple trajectories as they journey into the global environment.

As students interrogate the historical roots of racism, they also recognize the resistance movement to counter this, and the many parallels which can be found between Jamaican Blacks and African Americans. Excerpts from the biography, *My Friend Douglass* by Russell Freedman, provide the opportunity to strengthen our exploration of the resistance movement of African Americans and connect that to the resistance of the Maroons of Jamaica and to Black Lives Matter.

People of African Descent in the Americas: A Rich and Vibrant History of Resistance

Our investigation reveals that African descendants engaged in both passive and active resistance against slavery in the Americas. Interestingly, while Whites in the New World (The American Revolutionary War, 1775–1783) and in Europe declared their love of freedom, they engaged in the enslavement of millions of men and women of African descent. What is left out of the monolithic narrative is that Black activism during the Revolutionary War rose to a high pitch. Elizabeth Freeman (also known as Mum Bet) was one of several courageous slaves in America who filed freedom suits during the late 1700s as Black men and women used the principles of the American Revolution to challenge the institution of slavery. Though the system of slavery had positioned race relations in both North and South so that many Whites in northern states refused to accept free Blacks as equals, there were many active abolitionists—Black and White—who worked to subvert the system. This activism peaked at the time Congress passed the Fugitive Slave Law in 1850. Lewis Hayden is regaled in the narratives of Black history as an anti-slavery leader who had escaped from Kentucky into Canada with his family then later moved to Boston then New York. At a meeting of the Black community in 1850, he implored the audience to stand firm and united, unwavering in their resistance against the Fugitive Slave Laws. Frederick Douglass, meeting with this anti-slavery group, affirmed, "We must be prepared should this law be put into operation to see the streets of Boston running with blood (Collinson, 2000, p. 25). Further resistance including the writing and distribution of anti-slavery material, refusal to work, running away on the Underground Railroad, and the housing of runaway slaves became hallmarks of the creative response of Black people to their plight. Their innovative actions thwarted the slave laws in many forms of creative resistance, including Henry Brown who shipped himself to freedom in a wooden crate in 1850.

These are stories that reflect the breadth and depth of the resistance movement against slavery and racial injustice. Yet, this colorful history of resistance and survival in response to servitude is not included in the textbooks. My colleague Anne Bouie, whom I met at the 6th Annual Maroon conference in 2014, specializes in research on the resistance movement in the US colonies. In her exhibition, *A Loud Silence*, she asserted that exploring the enslavement period and the creative resistance of Blacks to the oppressive forces of colonialism points to the lies written by White slave owners and perpetuated in Eurocentric literature. First, that Africans were traumatized, demoralized, broken, and defeated by their survival on the death ships of the Middle Passage—the perilous journey across the Atlantic. Second, as a result of that experience, Africans and their descendants lost all memory of their former lives—their cultures, communities, social and political structures, and, most important, their spiritual and religious cosmologies, systems, rituals, and practices. Her work emphasizes how Africans and their descendants mounted effective resistance to enslavement.

In the 20th century, activism continued with struggle against new forms of injustices centralized in Jim Crow Laws and segregationist practices. The poignant picture of Rosa Park's stance of civil disobedience as she sat in the bus, refusing to move, becomes a metaphor of the Civil Rights Movement and the continuing struggle today. Martin Luther King, Jr., pointed out in his famous *I Have a Dream* speech that almost a hundred years after the Civil War was over Black men and women continued to fight hundreds of battles to win the same political, economic, and social rights that White Americans enjoyed. Today, the Black Lives Matter movement has become the 21st-century manifestation of the Civil Rights Movement.

Central to the oral tradition of Indigenous cultures, the stories of slave resistance, and the fight against discrimination, including those stories of Nanny of the Maroons and Paul Bogle, represent a well-articulated narrative of resistance that must be central to the creating of curriculum and pedagogy within global classrooms as tools to empower youth and assert their agency for change and transformation in the global village. When these stories are placed within the matrix of resistance throughout the globe, they rebuke the notion that rebellion was merely a spontaneous eruption in certain locales. Instead, they become woven into the fabric of a struggle that was transcontinental, waged across time and space, and which has a legacy that is celebrated within these communities. These stories emphasize the impact of colonialism worldwide to reveal how different groups of people have been subjugated and the ways in which they fought back against oppression. Used as classroom pedagogy, they bring forth the irrepressible nature of the people's activism and the enduring tenets of their culture. Sharing these stories is an excellent way to bring children's attention to the history, facts, and literature of Indigenous people that have been omitted from the books they use in school.

From Jamaica to the United States to Australia, these stories are every Black man's story, reminding us that we are united across the seas, land, and time; for our story is bound up in the memories we carved along the routes we have traveled into the Americas. I argue that these stories need to be officially recognized and inserted into the canon of world history and literature and pay homage to the profound influence of Africa on the socio-cultural fabric of the Americas.

Reflective Conversations: Question! Reflect! Write!

1. Research the life of Paul Bogle and create a comic strip or storyboard of his life leading up to his confrontation with Governor Eyre and his execution.
2. According to the author, what do Nanny of the Maroons and Paul Bogle have in common with Anansi the Spider?
3. Write to discuss your understanding of the passive and active ways Africans resisted oppression.

References

Brailsford, D. (2003). *The confessions of Anansi*. Kingston, Jamaica: LMH.

Collinson, G. (2011). Who claims me? In *A place at the table: The struggle for equal rights in America*. Retrieved from https://www.tolerance.org/classroom-resources/texts/who-claims-me

Craton, M. (1982). *Testing the chains: Resistance to slavery in the British West Indies*. Ithaca, NY: Cornell University Press.

Marshall, E. (2012). *Anansi's journey: A story of Jamaican cultural resistance*. Mona, Jamaica: University Press of the West Indies.

· 8 ·

CORRECTING HISTORY

Indigenous Children Writing Their Cultural Narratives

If you don't initiate the young, they will burn down the village to feel the heat.

—African Proverb

Students and teachers can think of examples in their own lives of stories passed down through oral tradition which have inspired them and served to validate their sense of personhood. These stories may be about a family member or a notable or humorous event, or may refer to an actual, fictional, or mythic event associated with a community, region, or institution. French author Danille Pennac (1992) wrote that we should make reading a gift we give to children and ourselves. The list he created of the 10 rights of the reader emphasizes the right to read anything one wishes or nothing at all. I wish to emphasize that our children have the right to hear their ancestral stories and share these with the rest of the world with their right to engage as they see fit. This book is part of the advocacy of freedom to read and tell one's stories. It is about speaking up to voice your perspective and validating who you are and what is important to you. It is about calling on the stories of your heritage to help you to reevaluate the world and your place in it. For as Philip Pullmon (2017) stated, after nourishment, shelter, and companionship, stories are the one thing we need most in the world.

Agents of Personal Transformation

According to socio-cultural theorists (Gee, 2002; Freire & Macedo, 1987) the school site is particularly significant in initiating change as it creates the space for social, historical, and cultural elements to intersect in expression of the way students experience the world. Over time, students begin to see threads of courage, ways in which their developing history might reveal examples of intentionality and perseverance. Thirteen-year-old Justin provides an interesting summary of the value of storytelling:

> *The telling of stories is important to African Americans because people like Frederick Douglass and Harriett Tubman teach and inspire people of our generation. Harriet freed over 300 slaves through the Underground Railroad and led them to Pennsylvania. This inspirational story taught us how strong and determined a woman can be. Frederick Douglass, a former slave, just like Harriet Tubman had an abusive mistress who refused to teach him to read and write, fortunately he found three white boys to teach him. Later on in his life, Abraham Lincoln invited Douglass to the podium during one of his speeches and titled him as one of his friends. Toward the end, Douglass wrote his autobiography.*

As students build their efficacy as cultural, custodial, and critical inquirers, their work presents a chorus of distinctive voices, each speaking with his/her own language. I ask them to identify and discuss the character traits exemplified by Nanny and then critically examine any similarities they might see between her and themselves.

In response to the question, *what makes Nanny a heroine?* Students personalize their perspective.

> *She fought for her rights no matter what the circumstances.*
>
> —Shawna-Lee

> *She was strong, brave and courageous; nobody got in her way.*
>
> —Ariel

> *She was willing to risk everything. She had confidence. I doubt myself at times. And I am not as strong as Nanny. But I am working on becoming a leader.*
>
> —Valerie

One student writes that while he is not a hero like Nanny, he believes that he is unique.

How am I unique? I am unique because I am one of the best soccer players on my team. I'm strong and quick and I got a strong kick. I average two goals a game at the least. My teammates and I have won many trophies because of our desire to win. But what makes me different is that I never give up and that I never want failure. Out of all my teammates, I believe I am truly the best. When we lose most of my teammates give up, but I always stay strong.

—Ryan

My students' engagement in the curriculum and pedagogy we construct communicates their developing subjectivities and critical consciousness and they weave poetry, biography, autobiography, drama, and the visual arts into their storytelling. We have come a long way on our journey in recognizing the significance of the oral traditions and their role in using diverse media in gathering and bringing these stories to life. These students have demonstrated that their stories are unique, interesting, and resistant to formula and they build academic capacity. Through raising their voices within this third space, students connect to each other, provide a portal into their cultural heritage, and extend an invitation to us to tap into their stories as classroom texts.

Teaching and learning is an active experience where we explore history, gather alternative stories from community members, and question and/or disrupt what has previously been presented as truth. This is classroom pedagogy that seeks to disrupt the tradition of failure asserted by statistics on the achievement gap and rewrite students' academic identity to reflect the rich cultural legacy of their cultural roots and topics on which they hold authority. With their permission, I insert my students' stories into classroom instruction and we examine and critique their texts in much the same way we do the texts from the traditional books and novels.

You are authors too, I tell my students. *I enjoyed reading this and the way you bring your culture alive. May I share this with the class?*

Invariably I get a resounding yes from students who are fascinated by the notion that they have something relevant to contribute to the classroom.

In April 2016 I take their work and a review of our developing collaboration to the American Education Research Association (AERA) annual convention, with their permission. As I prepare for the conference, my students participate in its construction, commenting and advising me on how to present.

You are doing too much talking, Valeria states. Show more pictures, especially of the Maroons. I think they would like that.

Remember to tell them about us, Sarai asserts. How we helped you with this. And make sure you tell them about Nanny of the Maroons catching the bullets in her butt. That's the interesting part.

And yes. I follow their instructions as their voices resonate in my head during the presentation. I include some of their artifacts and narratives in my presentation, feeling empowered by their display of agency in sharing their work, and uplifted with the scope to incorporate their funds of knowledge into classroom pedagogy.

I continue to emphasize my students' work as co-constructors of the curriculum I implement, learning from them and through them, and the art of teaching for social justice. It has been of particular interest to extend their understanding of African American heritage to include the Maroons of Jamaica and expose them to the role this group of people has played in the global movement towards freedom and democracy for all people. They are learning about the different ways in which oppressed people resisted and continue to resist, and their creative thrust towards community-building and affirmation of identity. Above all, they are acknowledging the power of their own voices, and as one youngster wrote, the capacity to accept the power of their agency and dream of a bright future:

I am a dreamer!
I dream to set a goal.
I dream to remind myself it is possible.
I dream to never give up.
Dreams are like marathons; you have to work hard to get to the top.
Without a dream, nothing will be achieved.
I am a dreamer!
—Natalie (Hispanic American)

Radicalizing Pedagogy

We must know deep in our bones and in our hearts that if the ancestors could survive the Middle Passage, we can survive anything.
—Isabel Wilkerson, *Essence* magazine, February 2015

Storytelling enables us to radicalize pedagogy and pursue alternative perspectives that take into account the diverse identities and needs that students bring to the classroom as well as the many gifts that are inherently situated in their life story. Radicalizing pedagogy is a thrust to make the curriculum alive, immediate; a constant stream of interaction between student and teacher, the environment and the community, the past and the present. It is a living testament to who we are as human beings living in an ever-changing world fostered by digital technology that enables us to connect across borders. Teaching an ancestral culture such as the Maroons of Jamaica and the Aboriginals of Australia has significant value in developing roots for ethnic identity and an extension of global awareness. They tell the story of how disenfranchised people find opportunities for creative resistance in marginalized spaces. This instructional methodology has brought us closer together, as well as engendering trust and helping me to reduce the sense of anxiety I have carried.

The process of undertaking this work has brought profound challenges. Even as I remain firm in my conviction that such stories offer hope to our children in school, this work is not without tension, and over the years, I have had to face the opposition of parents and educators who criticize the curriculum as ethnocentric. I realize that there are people who do not equate Afrocentric heritage with being American. I have had to argue and defend this work as pedagogy which enables students to critically and intellectually appraise curriculum material. I emphasize that the multicultural sources we utilize promote higher levels of cognitive activities and reading engagement. I have also had to emphasize both to the administration and parents that these literary events that are created within the classroom—rather than imposed from outside—are working to strengthen valued academic skills in analysis, interpretation, and application. I am committed to assert that exploring these stories provides us with an opportunity to engage in the shift in perspective about what is good literature; what should be in the classroom (Giroux, 1997).

While I agree that bringing these stories and artifacts into the classroom is not a panacea for solving the problem of educational inequity, I assert this approach as a viable step in addressing the problem and working towards decolonizing world literature. In highlighting these cultural practices of resistance against the violent and exploitative process of colonization, I am seeking to build historical awareness within the context of global education and deepen cross- cultural understanding of children's self-identity and experience (Giroux, 2001). For this has evolved into an engagement in a global dialogue on life-writing and the central role the oral tradition plays in the lives of

Indigenous people. Stories such as that of Nanny of the Maroons and Marcus' *Rite of Passage* are the threads that bind us together.

Cultural Literacy: Bringing Nanny Into 21st-Century Literacy

By using these stories to create a Third Space in the classroom, we are giving school children the opportunity to be creative in embedding their heritage in the narrative of schooling as they do in these assertions of name identity.

My parents named me Ryan because my great grandad was named Ryan. He was a military chief during World War 1. He was very strong, so that put him in battle and he was shot down by the enemies. But luckily he survived and soon after he met Lily who was my great grandmother. They both met at a service to honor those who died during the war. They got married and moved to Russia. They then decided to have a baby. His name was Ben, my grandad. The family then moved back to the USA, Chicago. At the age of 92, Ryan passed away leaving Ben fatherless and Lily at the age of 82. Ben got a wife and had a boy named Robert. Robert met my mom and they had me. My parents named me this because they saw the courage and strength in Ryan. So they named me Ryan because of his courage he shared throughout his life.

—Ryan

Malachi is the last chapter in the Old Testament. My mom and grandmother wanted a biblical name for me when my mother was pregnant. My grandmother wanted me to be Leviticus but my mother chose Malachi. Also, my dad wasn't happy about that because he wanted me to have the name Lynden the 111 (3rd). Out of all the names my mom chose Malachi because it means God's messenger. My parents' religion allowed me to have a biblical name. Knowing my name is powerful, I truly trust God with my life.

—Malachi

The name Mia means wished for child. It is of Latin origin. My mom and dad wanted to name me Mia but before that there was a lot of discussing. My mom and dad considered the name Isabella but a lot of people were naming their kids Isabella. My mom said why don't we name her Chloe? My dad didn't want to name me Chloe. My grandma always liked Mia. She suggested it and my mom and dad loved it. My dad also like the name Nicole so that became my middle name.

—Mia

The cultural space engendered in the classroom becomes fertile ground for students to explore and assert their identity, embedded within the threads of their home culture. In asserting their identity, the students are claiming their place within a wider world. It is my perspective that the depth of the students' involvement and engagement in discussions about identity, race, and equity has become my primary measure of success.

When we add the spice of our multicultural background into broader considerations of curriculum and pedagogy, we are likely to disrupt the normalization of our lives in school. Nanny's story can help to anchor a child experiencing the fluctuating levels of confidence that are part of growing up/adolescence. Such a story about one who succors strength to overcome adversity can help adolescents to develop the strength, knowledge, independence, and confidence needed to foster the journey towards adulthood. It can help youth to understand that adolescence can be challenging and that the world is not fair nor as simple as one might hope for. However, here are some directions one can take. Here is a story that shows you a route to determination and perseverance. This anchoring of the student as a valuable member of the classroom community, this elevation of the student's voice, goes a long way towards creating an effective student who is critically conscious of his/her location within this cultural space.

Traits of an Effective Student

1. Inquisitive, inquiring—asks questions to expand his/her perspective.
2. Participatory—participates in classroom discourse and seeks to contribute to the development of multiple perspectives and an extended worldview.
3. Innovative—utilizes digital media to bring together powerful ideas with words, images, and personal storylines that contribute to building a literary legacy of the unique and significant contributions of one's culture.

Traits of an Effective Teacher

1. Interrogates him/herself and recognizes what he/she needs to become effective in a particular context.
2. Examines oneself—biases and prejudices—and is agentive about addressing them.

3. Knows and understands the history on unequal schooling and is committed to becoming an agent of change.
4. Recognizes the need to have critical friends and takes action to secure such friends.
5. Extends pedagogy to incorporate students' funds of knowledge.

Reflective Conversations: Question! Reflect! Write!

1. What qualities does Nanny possess that make her a heroine? Are there any particular qualities with which you can personally identify?
2. How do the sensory details of the description of Nanny's community influence your perspective of that particular community?
3. In psychology, anything a person does is called behavior. Behavior has two causes: heredity and environment. Heredity refers to what a person has when he or she is born. Environment refers to a person's surroundings and his/her experiences. A person learns new behaviors through the experiences in the environment. Based on what you have learned about Nanny, to what extent do you think that she was shaped by the environment? Do you think that her actions were based on heredity or the environment?

References

Freire, P., & Macedo, D. (1987). *The politics of education: Culture, power and liberation*. South Hadley, MA: Bergin & Garvey.

Gee, P. A. (2001). Identity as an analytic lens for research in education. *Review of Research in Education, 25*, 99–125.

Gee, J.P. (2002). A sociocultural perspective on early literacy development. In S. Neuman and D. Dickinson (Eds.), Handbook of early literacy research (pp. 30–353). New York: Guilford.

Giroux, H. (1997). *Pedagogy and the politics of hope: Theory, culture, and schooling*. Boulder, CO: Westview Press.

Giroux, H. (2001). *Theory and resistance in education: Towards a pedagogy for the opposition*. Westport, CT: Bergin & Garvey.

Pennac, D. (1992). The rights of the reader. Somerville, MA: Candlewick Press.

Pulman, P. (2017). Daemon voices: Essays on storytelling. Oxford, UK: David Fickling Books.

PART III
VIEWING THE CURRICULUM
THROUGH AN
ANTI-COLONIAL LENS

PREAMBLE TO PART III:
VIEWING THE CURRICULUM
THROUGH AN ANTI-COLONIAL LENS

We Want Land, Bread, Housing, Education, Clothing, Justice and Peace
—Black Panther Platform & Program, 1966

I tend to view my genealogy through a series of metaphors, and land plays a central role in the assertion of my identity. The land has always loomed large in my consideration of family and family history and I am therefore able to make ready connections to its significant value to the Maroons of Jamaica and the disenfranchised who wander across the globe today seeking a place of refuge. As a child I was lured by the geography of the house in which I was born; my grandmother's house where I spent my childhood summers; my mother's sisters' houses where I visited, played, and argued with my cousins. Even when we moved away there was always something about the land that was like a siren calling to me. I was attracted to it and repelled by it at the same time. On one hand, there was something familiar and comforting about the annual summer homecoming at my grandmother's. During the day, we played hopscotch in the yard with the children from the village. I loved the coziness of my grandmother's large bedroom where several of us would sleep at nights. And I loved waking up to warm bread and bizzy tea in the mornings. Yet, on the other hand, the place also seemed remote and intimidating. My grandparents, their siblings, and their fore-parents are buried on this land. As a child we played on the graves during the day; but as it got dark, I became a little scared of the ghosts that my older brother said came out each night.

This is the land which roots me to my ancestry. It reminds me that I have a place to call home. It speaks to me of my family connection. It is located in a community which resounds with the nuances of my Afrocentric heritage. Black and brown skin Jamaicans. Patois-speaking locals whose words vibrate with the natural rhythms of the land. The flora that encircles the red dirt that calls us back to the earth. All of these elements form an intricate web that brings coherence to my life regardless of my location and circumstances. I am always able to make a circuitous journey back into the wellspring of this legacy, whether through physical temporal time or spiritual liminal space via genetic memory.

Chamberlin (1995, p. 108) asserted that the language of memory is the means by which tradition is transmitted; the means by which structure and values are internalized, passed on, and inherited. This is the place where the seeds of storytelling were sewn. It is here that we would gather at night and tell stories and recite poems and improvise verbal rhythms (called spoken-word poetry today) as we went along, competing with each other to see who could out-talk the other. This is the place where my grandmother shared the legacy of Nanny of the Maroons and shaped my life forever. This land, acres of red dirt first purchased by my great grandfather in 1865, anchors me to my history and my lineage, one that is rooted in storytelling and the colorful traditions of Africa.

Holding Steadfast to Our Stories

Estes (1992) admonished that the best way to escape horror is to create your way out of it. The oral sources from which sprung the stories of Nanny of the Maroons and many of the heroes of Indigenous cultures are vital to the continuing survival of our people. We utilize these stories as a pedagogy of courage in contesting the empirical evidence provided in Western scholarship about our historical background. Mary Chamberlin (1995) stated

> oral sources are neither true nor false, and to pursue them as either is to pursue a chimera. What is needed is an interrogation of oral sources to arrive at a different set of historical evidence that historicize Black people across the globe (p. 108).

Memories, she confirmed, are imaginative recounting, representative of a set of meanings by which and through which lives are interpreted and transmitted, constructed and changed. She continued, "Rather than relegate gender and memory to the edge of history, they should be foregrounded as one of a set of central, interpretive tools for understanding the nature and process of historical change" (p. 108).

Global Entanglements and Maroon Cultural Heritage

For people of color worldwide, our traumatic past continues to exert an impact on the present as the legacies of colonialism return again and again to dominate our stories. Yet, we are motivated in our recognition that these pasts can also inspire rich creativity as a past remembered, challenged, and remade through our own efforts and told with our voice. The interplay of fact and fiction that informs my accounting of Nanny of the Maroons helps to emphasize and balance the ideology of brotherhood and the communal consciousness of Indigenous people; positioning us as empowered members of a community of practice.

While the Caribbean has been an agonizing battleground for contending histories and cultural interpretations, the Maroons' location on their sovereign lands in Jamaica represents an anti-colonial stance in talking back to history. Since their acquisition of the land in 1739, they have established their own historical conditions of citizenship on Maroon land. The indomitable spirit of the Jamaican Maroons led them to thwart all attempts to penetrate their strongholds. They fought ferociously, utilizing guerilla tactics in such a manner that they were never conquered by the British. The onslaught of their resistance movement led to a significant disruption of the sugar economy in Jamaica and undermined its profitability, propelling the movement towards the end of slavery. This stance of resistance remains central to the enduring revolutionary movement throughout the Diaspora. The Maroons are comprised largely of Blacks from the Gold Coast region of Africa (known today as Ghana), captured and administered through the slave holding in Koromantyn, who became identified as Coromantees. The Coromantees developed a reputation for their expertise in warfare and their fighting spirit. Challenged by the hegemony of the slave plantation, maroonage became a way of life and guerilla warfare the chief strategy of the Maroons. Calling on the spirit of their ancestors, they adapted to their location and strategically utilized its resources in unison with their skills and knowledge to create a counter-hegemonic system that challenged, baffled, and outmaneuvered the British imperial forces and won against them in the First Maroon War of 1739 and the Second Maroon War of 1796.

Theirs is not an artificial extension of European history projected as the New World, but a fusion of ancient Africa with the present location; a contemporary articulation of citizenship connected to and expressed through the geographical metaphor of rootedness and belonging within the African Diaspora. The Maroons have aligned themselves with the natural environment of the Jamaican landscape, utilizing their folk knowledge of flora and fauna, their cultural beliefs and history, to enhance their lives (Semali & Kincheloe, 2002, p. 3) and create and maintain a system that is adaptable, growing, and changing over time. In peaceful living today, their heritage is just as pronounced as it was in the 18th century. Their Indigenous methods used to maintain their cultural retentions and resist the thrust of Imperialism inform us that there are alternative ways of life; that communal living still has a place in the 21st century despite the Western assertion of capitalism.

The preservation of this way of life, however, is not without threats and the Maroons are challenged to implement critical and creative responses to the encroachment of contemporary developments on their way of life. Of the several Maroon leaders I have interviewed, all conveyed a deep concern about the threat to maintaining the strength of the community. Colonel Williams and the late Frank Lumsden spoke of the pervading influence of urban culture and the media. The preservation of the Maroon culture and ideology rests heavily on the tenets of intergenerational teaching which they consider will be influenced by youth responding to the urban call, leaving the communities to locate in cities in urban Jamaica, including Kingston and Montego Bay. Further, the Maroons' philosophy of sworn secrecy of the sacred details of their African heritage prevents an open broadcast of the wellspring of their heritage. The limited educational facilities on Maroon land is yet another major factor. There are only seven schools throughout the Maroon communities, (elementary and junior high schools) and so youth have to leave to go elsewhere for further education. This migration results in cultural erosion and a depletion of the population of the Maroon communities.

The leaders rely on the strength of their cultural practices to retain and maintain the integrity of their ancient cultural heritage. There is a heavy reliance on intergenerational teaching practices to ensure that youth are socialized into the ideology of Maroonage and that they have the knowledge base and historical consciousness needed to root them in the stronghold of their African heritage. Language, music, storytelling, including folklore, have been central to the forging and maintaining of the Maroon identity; the forging of a group identity molded from the clay of Afro-ethnicity and their creative response in acclimating to the geography of the new location, the force of oppression, and the intermingling of diverse ethnicities from Africa.

The Maroons have asserted the ideology of being your brother's keeper in their commitment in placing community above individuality; a community that supports connection and caring relationships. This agency pushed them to establish a communal lifestyle which consolidated their reciprocal relationship with the land. Scholars have noted that their attachment to the land and their African heritage was a major factor in their resistance and survival (Bilby, 2005). Even as they demonstrate an incredible ability to adapt and change over time, the land remains at the core of their spirituality; a force that sustains, and is sustained by, the community of people and their culture. They have made a significant contribution to transatlantic Black consciousness through music, dance, and religion in a manner that has worked successfully to disrupt the divide between classes and rigid social structure in Jamaica. The Maroons' assertion of their African heritage has deeply impacted the cultural landscape of Jamaican culture including Reggae music, Rastafari religion, and the Revivalist religion. In short, the Maroons' influence has touched upon all aspects of Jamaican life, through creative expressions as well as broad social changes.

My experience on Maroon land revealed their incredible commitment to engage in rituals and performances dedicated to protecting cultural material that is sacred and significant. With little-to-no crime reported in their history, they demonstrate the value of prioritizing connection, belonging, healing, and restoration rather than the blame, alienation, and punishment so characteristic of capitalist societies. Colonel Williams, leader of the Accompong Maroons, noted, for example, that since the Maroons settled on their sovereign land more than 277 years ago, only one petty crime of theft has been committed. Considering the state of crisis that grips our current society, with crime, social discontent, and alienation, it seems clear that there is much that the rest of the world could learn from Maroon society, beginning with the island of Jamaica itself where the Maroons of this study are located. It should become an important objective to explore issues and practices of Indigenous peoples such as the Maroons across the globe and determine how we may learn ways of peaceful living from them. For this form of cultural heritage, the people's total ways of living passed from one generation to another, is an invaluable resource for our global community. Yet, the super powers of the globe continue to ignore this rich resource within our midst and continue to undermine, ignore, or exploit Indigenous people. The United Nations stated that there are 370 million Native peoples living in this world. When the *UN Declaration on the Rights of Indigenous Peoples* was issued and adopted during the 62nd session at the UN Headquarters in New York City, September 13, 2007, the United States, New Zealand, Australia, and Canada voted against it, saying they could not support it because of concerns over provisions on self-determination, land, and resources rights (UNESCO, 2015b, p. 3). This report goes on to emphasize that ignorance or concealment of major historical events constitutes an obstacle to mutual understanding, reconciliation, and cooperation among peoples.

The truth is, Indigenous people's wealth of knowledge includes the cultural capital of strategies to live in harmony with the land and to preserve it for generations to come. All across the globe, they share a similar worldview on man's relationship with the land. Both Maroon and Aboriginal elders who I have interviewed emphasize their symbiotic relationship with the land. They note that non-Indigenous people and landowners might consider land as something they own, a commodity to be bought and sold, an asset to derive profit from, and also a means to make a living off or simply a place to make a home. For Indigenous people the relationship is much deeper. The land owns Indigenous people, and every aspect of their lives is connected to it. Theirs is a profound spiritual connection to the land. Aboriginal author Gilbert (1977) shared, for example, that Aboriginal law and spirituality are intertwined with the land, the people, and creation, and this forms their culture and sovereignty. The health of land and water is central to their culture. The Land is their mother, a life force to whom they are accountable which gives them the responsibility to care for it.

The Maroon Communities of Jamaica

There are five major Maroon communities in Jamaica. Each has been established based on the treaty secured by Maroon leaders in the 18th century. Each community is governed by a colonel who is elected and assisted by a Maroon council of 24 elected members. The land they occupy is at the core of their spirituality and communal living. Each village holds an annual celebration that honors the founding fathers and mother (Queen Nanny) of their community and is enmeshed within the roots of their African heritage. UNESCO spoke of the importance of breaking the silence about the history of slavery (UNESCO, 2015a) and the value of Indigenous heritage. In its *Declaration of the Decade of Indigenous People*, the organization noted that the study of Indigenous people and the move to break the silence regarding the slave trade and the cultural heritage of Indigenous people is a move towards reconciliation and understanding of the great upheavals which inscribed the shaping of contemporary society. The spirituality and communal living enacted on Maroon land is testimony to the culture of peace the organization references as it speaks to the urgency of promoting reflection on cultural pluralism, intercultural dialogue, and the construction of new identities and citizenships. UNESCO's recognition of the Moore Town Maroons' Koromantyn language, the Ashante dialect of the Akran region of Ghana, as one of the masterpieces of the oral and intangible heritage of humanity, and the designation of Accompong Village as a cultural site, certainly reinforce the perspective that the Maroons continue to bequeath a legacy to the global community.

> *The heroes of a nation embody its cherished values, expresses its highest purposes, and inspires its noblest achievements.*
>
> —Sir Phillip Sherlock

The Maroons' way of life stands up to contemporary representations of capitalism to reaffirm the philosophy of a community in sustainable living with the land. This is a community that asserts its determination to enact its cultural retentions and, through intergenerational relationships, bequeath to future generations their ancestral/sovereign land, their system of government, and their African-ethnic identity as the basis of their continued existence as a people. Like other native peoples across the globe, including Native Americans and Aboriginals, they hold steadfast to the perspective that humans are but stewards of the land and that their experience with the land is both temporal and non-linear. "Where they have maintained a close living relationship to the land, there exists a co-operative attitude of give and take, a respect for the Earth and the life it supports, and a perception that humanity is but one of many species" (Burger, 1990, p. 1). This shared perspective is instrumental in constructing a borderless society knitting Indigenous people together, demonstrating that interdependence is a basic element of human society and its survival.

References

Bilby, K. (2005). *True born Maroons*. Orlando, FL: University Press of Florida.

Burger, J. (1990). Indigenous people. Retrieved from UNESCO website: http://www.unesco.org/education/tlsf/mods/theme_c/popups/mod11t01s02.html#1

Chamberlain, M. (1995). Gender & memory: Oral history & women's history. In V. Shepherd, B. Brereton, & B. Bailey (Eds.), *Engendering history: Caribbean women in historical perspective*. New York, NY: St. Martin's Press.

Estes, C. P. (1992). *Women who run with the wolves: Myths & legends of the wild woman archetype*. New York, NY: Ballantine Books.

Gilbert, K. (1977). *Living Black: Blacks talk to Kevin Gilbert*. Ringwood, Australia: Penguin Books.

Semali, L. M., & Kincheloe, J. (Eds.). (2002). *What is Indigenous knowledge? Voices from the academy*. New York, NY: Routledge.

UNESCO. (2015a). *International decade for people of African descent (2015–2024)*. Retrieved from http://en.unesco.org/decade-people-african-descent

UNESCO. (2015b). *Teaching and learning for a sustainable future*. Retrieved from http://www.unesco.org/education/tlsf/mods/theme_gs/mod0a.html

FROM AFRICA TO THE NEW WORLD

The Sustainable Maroon Communities of Jamaica

Freedom is never voluntarily given by the oppressor, it must be demanded by the oppressed.
—Martin Luther King, Jr.

The Planters Did Not Tame the Slaves or Deflect Their Will to Freedom (Craton, 1982)

Craton (1982) stated that the Maroons provided an admired example for rebellious slaves. The Maroon wars cost the colonial regime a quarter million pounds and hundreds of men killed. "For the plantocracy the war was a constant drain of money and men without prospect of victory in the field" (Craton, 1982, p. 87). In 1796, following the Second Maroon War, where the Maroons emerged victorious after a 5-month onslaught, the Assembly of the Government of Jamaica issued this report, *"The faid Captain Cudjoe, the reft of his captains, adherents, and men, fhall be forever hereafter in a perfect flate of freedom and liberty"* (Jamaica Assembly, 1796). The proceedings also note that the Maroons, *"were not reducible by any regular plan of attack,"* and that they carried out attacks against the British as if they had nothing to lose *"except life and a wild and favage freedom"* (ix, p. 14).

These words are etched in history, reinforcing the treaty with the *mighty* British government which was forced to acknowledge the power of the Maroons in 1739, revealing their own vulnerability. This emphasizes the magnitude of the Maroons' onslaught on the British Empire, for as Bilby (2005) stated, the Maroons had a powerful impact on pushing the British to end slavery with the First Maroon War in 1739 and the Second Maroon War in 1795. Much of their success seems to have been reinforced by their intuitive leadership and the inherent understanding of the value of succoring strength from the generations of warriors who preceded them. These warriors "melded traditions of resistance both from the Amerindians, whom they largely replaced, and from their own African forbear" (Craton, 1982, p. 13). And today, they continue to hand down intuition from generation to generation, fostered by a commitment to enacting rituals that involve the entire community of practice, from children to elders. These rituals support them in remaining "in possession of instinctual powers, insight, intuition, endurance, tenacious living, keen sensing, far vision, acute hearing, singing over the dead, intuitive healing and tending to the creative fires" (Estes, 1992, p. 197).

The Maroon towns of Accompong, Moore Town, Trelawny Town, Scotts Hall, and Charles Town together form a community of practice which offers exemplary standards of social solidarity; a community of practice which uses rituals as one way to put their lives in perspective (Estes, 1992). Nanny and her brothers, Accompong, Cudjoe, Johnny, and Quao defiantly fled the plantation and hid in the Blue Mountains area of northern Saint Thomas Parish, then strategically organized themselves to take up leadership in selected terrains across Jamaica; self-organizing and adaptable to the landscape. Amid the onslaught of hegemony of the plantocracy they adapted themselves to the terrain and the terrible circumstances of being hunted by the British. Cudjoe journeyed to Saint James Parish and organized Cudjoe Town; Accompong settled in Saint Elizabeth Parish and set up Accompong Town; Nanny founded Nanny Town and, later, established Moore Town with Quao, who eventually became her successor. In recognition of the greater connection of their work to the broader ideals of freedom, they utilized guerilla tactics to structure and defend their new habitat. These sites were strategically located in the dense rain forests high above sea level, and largely inaccessible. There was heavy reliance on the contours of each location to protect the warriors and support them in their war against the well-equipped British. These strategic moves exemplify the possibilities of alternative methods of protest and collective action (Kocher, 2002; Preston, 1997) that is such an integral part of New World development from slavery to Emancipation to Jim Crow and the Civil Rights Movement through to contemporary times, including Black Lives Matter, when the world is crying out for the same justice and equality that our ancestors fought for. The Maroons worked in harmony with the land and wrestled freedom from the oppressor. They persevered with relentless resistance buoyed by the agency of their cultural heritage and established a commitment to freedom which remains at the core of the Jamaican society and a beacon for others throughout the region.

It is said that during the 150 years that the Maroons fought imperialism, they were buoyed by the spirit of Nanny and her commitment to freedom. From Nanny they have learned the value of enacting strategy and nurturing the soul as vital elements of survival. In my interpretation and understanding of Maroon historiography I see great value in their transformative ritual celebration of the spiritual existence of being human in a time of savage injustice against their humanity. In keeping with Freire (1970), they highlight the power of a people's convictions and the capacity of grassroots leadership to resist oppression, and, through the sheer force of their indomitable will embodied in their cultural agency, resist the pressure of the oppressor in a manner which forces the oppressor to strike a bargain. The British colonial authorities recognized the power of the Maroons and conceded their autonomy, written into history and honored today, in keeping with the *United Nations Declaration of the Rights of Indigenous people*.

Nanny Town/Moore Town: The Historical Authority of Queen Nanny

Yvonne Knight Thomas, teacher at Rio Grande Junior High in Moore Town, speaks of the empowering effects that the heritage of the Maroon culture has on the children who attend the school and live in the community. She has brought a group of children to the 8th Annual Maroon conference at Asafu Yard, Jamaica, where they recite poetry that speaks to the history of Maroonage and the ways in which this has shaped the community. In a colorful presentation, spoken in Jamaican Maroon creole and anchored in the rhythmic beat of the Jamaican vernacular, the children evoke the sensibilities of Queen Nanny as a matriarch and a spiritual guide, reminding the audience of the need to take care of the land and preserve it through sustainable care for generations to come. Principal Kathleen Wright, also in attendance, speaks with me about the central positioning of heritage within the curriculum. From our conversation I discern that Nanny has become a post-colonial allegory for the school children and the community; one whose influence remains tangible and celebrated, spiritual and reverential. "The children carry a consciousness of their background, the long history of their Maroon culture with them," she tells me. And I can readily see this as they perform with certitude, engaging the audience in a performance that is rooted in history and a consciousness of contemporary developments, extolling the audience of the repercussions of littering and pollution; reminding us that Queen Nanny maintains a watchful vigil over the community.

These school children, like the other citizens of Moore Town, speak a variant of Koromante (derived from the name of the slave port Koromantyn in Ghana) blended within the Jamaican Maroon creole. Music and drumming are elevated within their presentations and they extoll the virtues of story-telling, engaging the listeners in their narrative reconstruction of a past that esteems their present. Like their elders, these children have become part of the discipline of connecting to the archetypal image of Nanny, tapping into a resource that transcends the present, informing them that they belong to something much larger than themselves. Queen Nanny rises up as the myth-ical archetype that knits the community together, and these children evoke her presence with a calm certitude that is inspiring.

Folding into the essence of the spiritual archetypal authority of Queen Nanny, I am reminded of the words of Dr. Estes (1992), who stated that storytelling comprises narratives which reflect the history of how people perceive themselves, elevating the tiny corners of their life to prominence. Throughout the day, from the presenters to the audience, to the vendors at booths and the children performing and those attending, I hear the repe-tition of symbolic language that lies at the heart of Maroon culture. This is language that symbolizes the continuation of the community, from the Leeward Maroons to the Windward Maroons, all of whom are represented, including Maroon chief Colonel Grizzle (Scotts Hall), Maroon scholar and documentarian Roy Anderson, and Gaaman Mama G, First Female Saamaca Gaaman, International Maroon Queen, who conducts a libation to evoke the presence of Queen Nanny, who she says is her principal guide in her role as international leader of the Maroons. Mama G offers a libation to the ancestral spirits, sprinkling White Rum to the four corners of the earth, and asserts that Queen Nanny has passed on both the principles of strategic leadership and communion with the land to Indigenous people all over the world. "She valued the complexity of the land and embraced the Earth, welcoming its resources as part of her military strategy and intuitive leadership." Gaaman Mama G emphasizes that the political power wielded by Nanny was deeply sustained by her connection to the land. She notes that as a ritualist specialist, she could inspire her people to take actions that were heroic in the eyes of the community. Based on Estes (1992), Nanny seems to have developed a relationship with the *wildish nature* as an essential part of woman's individuation.

Gloria Simms, International Maroon Queen

"There is an obeah woman in every Maroon community in Sierra Leone," she states, referencing the settlement of Jamaican Maroons who were forcibly removed from Jamaica and relocated in Nova Scotia by the British who deceitfully negated the agreement of the Second Maroon War, 1795. According to the Maroons of Jamaica, the British invited the Maroons to a celebration dinner to confirm the new peace agreement, then apprehended them and put them on a ship to Nova Scotia. From Nova Scotia, the Maroons journeyed to Sierra Leone where they established themselves as leaders and set up a community based on their heritage and the way of life of the Maroon communities in Jamaica. In harnessing the history of the Maroons and centering Nanny as a multifaceted feminist leader, Mama G. references the multiple cultural voices of Maroonage from across the globe and emphasizes how their worlds today are an outgrowth of a complex history, and the day's celebration a symbolization of its continuity. "We honor Queen Nanny for her determination, her fighting spirit and the way she has empowered the people at Pumpkin Hill," she intones before breaking into a spiritual dance. These ritualistic enactments and celebration have become an intricate ecology of African-centered rituals, which tie the communities together from across the vast ranges of the Jamaican landscape and the African Diaspora.

The leaders of the community and Maroons presenting at the conference and those leading workshops or hosting booths all reiterated this worldview of the historical empowerment of the Maroons. As anthologized in the Pumpkin Hill lore, Nanny understood the complexity of the land and its central role in the lives of her people. She embraced the land as an ally and used it strategically to empower her people and engage the oppressors in fearsome battle. She paid homage to Asase Ya, the Earth Mother of the Ashanti of Western Africa, and called upon her for protection and provision of all they needed: water, food, shelter, and a resting place after death. She utilized herbs and plants to heal and sustain the health of her people, a practice which further esteemed her among them.

The local storytellers corroborate this information, which is also confirmed by the Jamaica Information Service (2015). By 1720 Nanny and Quao had settled and controlled a large area in the most inaccessible region of the Blue Mountains. The community was organized with Nanny as the political and military leader who inspired her followers and trained them in the art of guerilla warfare and in strategies to raid plantations, secure food and weapons, and entice slaves to join them. They planted herbs and crops and bartered provisions from the land in the neighboring communities and slave markets for goods they needed and weapons for fighting. One legend has it that during a time of great challenge, when the Maroons lacked sufficient food for survival, the ancestors visited Nanny during her sleep and gave her pumpkins seeds which she planted, and she was subsequently able to feed her people from the pumpkins that sprang up. Nanny's ability to grow pumpkins from magical seeds given to her by her ancestors serves as a metaphor for perseverance and survival (Craton, 1982, p. 226).

Intentional in living in freedom, she organized the village as a family structure based on the tenets of communal living, resembling village life in Ghana. This site of citizenship for free Blacks assumed symbolic value as well as becoming a beacon of hope and a monument to the ideals of freedom. In 1734 the British attacked and destroyed Nanny Town in a 5-day battle where approximately 80 British soldiers and an unknown number of Maroons were killed. Nanny then went east and founded New Nanny Town on the slopes of the John Crow Mountains. New Nanny Town later became Moore Town in 1739 after the peace treaty. By then, her followers were divided into two groups. One went with her to New Nanny Town (Moore Town), and the other went with her brother Quao to Crawford Town. (Crawford Town was later organized into the current Charles Town). After the peace treaty, it was later given the name New Nanny Town, and consisted of the 500 acres of land granted to them. Nanny requested more land from the British, and in 1781, Nanny Town was extended when Muretown, consisting of an additional 1270 acres, was added. The current Moore Town is derived from this coupling of these lands. Though it remains unclear if their brotherhood was formed in warriorship or if, in fact, they were blood siblings, Cudjoe, Quao, Cuffy, and Nanny all hailed from the Ashanti area of West Africa and became the first group of African Jamaicans to fight for, and gain, their freedom from the colonial forces in the New World.

Nanny Town was strategically poised over Stony River via a 900-foot ridge, making a surprise attack by the British practically impossible. The Maroons at Nanny Town also organized look-outs for such an attack as well as designated warriors who could be summoned by the sound of the Abeng. Osen (2014) spoke of Nanny Town as possibly the most sacred of all Maroon sites; a large village of over 149 houses, central to the preservation of their African ancestry. It was from this strategically located stronghold that Nanny launched her wars against the colonial government, establishing it as a site of community citizenship, authenticity, and power.

Guerilla Warfare: Destabilizing the Plantocracy

Nanny utilized guerilla warfare as the strategy against the British. Through her system of surprise attack and camouflage, she cunningly out-maneuvered the British and thwarted their efforts to attack the Maroons despite the latter's lack of weaponry. Oral history recounts that Nanny herself would cover her soldiers with branches and leaves, instructing them to stand as still as possible so that they would resemble trees. As the British soldiers approached, completely unaware that they were surrounded, they would swiftly be picked off by the Maroons. These memories are rooted in the narrative of Maroon ideology and the broader political landscape of Jamaica, recalling their history of resistance and the agency of their ancestors.

Nanny's philosophy of resistance, subterfuge, and emancipation continues to influence diverse populations across the Americas, connecting diverse groups, establishing relations between the various forms of oppression. Powerful myths and legends passed down by word of mouth over the centuries assert her power and authority and the enduring influence on the lives of people of color in the New World. From the mists of these legends, Nanny Town emerges as sacred space for the Maroons, a place of belonging to be treated with love and respect. Nanny responded to the utopian impulse; that instinct to be free and autonomous. It is said, according to Jamaican lore, that her powers were beyond compare. She would prepare charms meant to kill, to heal, or to make oneself be the object of someone's affection. Placed at the head of the armies, she encouraged them with her dances, chants, and invo-cations. Local legend also shares that Nanny could turn into an invisible bird to spy upon the enemy and strike them from a distance.

Nanny's warriorship is highly regaled in the folklore of Jamaica among Maroons and non-Maroons alike as her story is indelibly encrypted within the ancestral writings of the community. Her grave is revered as an ancestral site, resting atop a lonely hill in Moore Town, close to New Nanny Town and Pumpkin Hill (the site where she harvested the pumpkins). The site remains wild and uncultivated, reminding us of her relentless struggle against oppres-sion, acknowledging that indeed, she was buried in a free land, despite the continuation of slavery at the time. This sacred site invokes the words of abo-litionist and poet, Francis E. W. Harper (1825–1911), whose ancestral writing almost a century after Nanny's death, like the folklore of the Maroons today, knit Black people together across the annals of history, upholding our most fervent desire to live and be buried in a free land.

Sharpe (2003) stated that, "renditions of Nanny's life are nonetheless grounded in and of the authority that the historical woman possessed" (p. 5). Moore Town Maroons and their descendants credit Nanny not only with founding the earliest Maroon settlements, but also with developing ingenious methods for their continuous growth and survival in the 21st century (Rucker, 2015). Today, there are a little more than 1,000 Maroons living on the eco-sus-tainable land of Moore Town. These stalwart descendants of Queen Nanny have been recognized by UNESCO (2003) for maintaining the Koromantyn language of Ghana, "a masterpiece of the Oral and Intangible Heritage of Humanity," and in particular, the retention of the Koromantyn Play inscribed with the Akan language of ancient Africa.

The symbolic resonance of this courageous woman is conveyed nation-wide through her portrait etched on the $500 bill of Jamaica, where she is a national heroine of great stature. Her people's perspective of her cultural significance is no doubt strengthened by the presence of her portrait embla-zoned at the Gilder Lehrman Center for the Study of Slavery, Resistance, and Abolition at Yale University. Nannyville Gardens, a residential community located in Kingston, Jamaica, was founded in the 1970s. There is a spiritual resonance in this story of this diminutive Black woman who stood up to the giant of imperialism, helped to bring slavery to an end, and continues to shape the movement towards freedom today.

Charles Town Asafu Yard: Stories and Metaphors

Rodney Rose blows the abeng, called the Jebry in Maroon language, a ritual tradition to signal the start of the gathering and celebration in Asafu Yard, Charles Town, 2016. The abeng, a wind instrument fashioned from the cow horn, has been used throughout the centuries to convey complex messages across far distances and was especially important to signal the beginning of battle during slavery. Its use is also extended to communicate across long distances, call meetings and gatherings to order, and also to let the community know that there are outsiders entering. (Non-Indigenous people were not allowed into the Maroon communities prior to 1986). The abeng is a symbol of communication that exemplifies the diverse and creative means of communication. Nanny and the other Maroons of Jamaica used it to communicate across the land and confound their oppressors.

Scholars have come from all over the world and local people and children are also here to acknowledge this event as a celebration of their life's history, an occasion where the community comes together to interact with the visitors and demonstrate the veracity of the age-old story of their lineage. Each time I have visited Asafu Yard (meeting and celebration place) in Charles Town, I have been inspired by the sense of authority enacted by the Maroons of this town, which was established in the 1700s by their rebel leader. The town was developed as a new settlement of Crawford Town with the group of Maroons who had split from Nanny's group following the end of the First Maroon War and the signing of the peace treaty, before moving down to this area in Buff Bay, Portland. This story remains a source of enduring pride for them as they readily recount their history and culture. Scholars (Bilby, 2005; Sherlock & Bennett, 1998) have noted that their ancestors' resistance to slavery is of great importance to 21st-century Maroons, who place great value on the traditions of Africa and its culture to their existence.

Colonel Frank Lumsden, elected leader of the Charlestown Maroons, emphasized that agency earlier at the 6th Annual Maroon conference. "We have to invest in and safeguard the economic development of our community. This is our strength and the most important tool we can call upon to build on the legacy of our ancestors." He revealed a deep perception of social norms and knowledge of the community's socio-political development and described the Maroons' use of the natural heritage of the area, the forests and the streams and the waterfalls, to develop and establish their legacy. "They wielded battles and won wars," he asserted, noting how these warriors utilized the Blue Mountains and John Crow Mountains as allies in their guerilla war-fare. He was firm in protecting the legacy of the Maroon community even as he upheld the national laws of Jamaica.

During our interviews, which took place from 2012 to 2014, he asserted the resiliency of the Maroon people and their focus on preserving the cultural legacies of their African roots. Maroon communities such as this community of practice operate as a self-governing entity, influenced by their past leaders' philosophy of independence and empowerment. This continues to shape their operation, especially the cultural traditions. The objects and cultural arti-facts the Maroons display in the museum or on walls provide a visual memo-rial of their journey from Africa, across the Middle Passage, onto the land they now reside, negotiated and acquired through peace treaties during the 18th century.

In exploring Charles Town, I discovered examples of the ties that bind their common humanity. I engaged with the community members in a narra-tive that brought to the fore the creativity of the region and raised questions regarding Caribbean cultural identity and the global community. I observed Maroon children integrally involved within the cultural fabric of their com-munity making clear their agency as transmitters of their culture. For the Maroons who are culturally rooted in the land, eco-Indigenous knowledge has been a key development resource in the community and a central part of their identity. Marcia Douglas-Kim, herbalist and basic school teacher, explained, "Our Maroon heritage has provided us with the tools to heal our-selves and move our generation forward." This ecological consciousness is of great significance to the Maroons, who regard the land as sacred because "the ancestors are buried on these grounds. The land provides us with plants for cures, spells, infections. The Pepper elder-plant for example, protects the gastro-intestinal track and is used in the popular jerk spice," Douglas-Kim asserted.

Those Wild and Savage Negroes

At the 2016 annual conference, Sharon White from the University of the West Indies reviewed the development of the Charles Town Maroons, noting how the leadership council had engaged in a program of economic devel-opment utilizing human capital and the resources of the land to build the community in a manner which maintained the integrity of its ancestral roots. She spoke of the leadership's awareness and acknowledgement of the need to respond to the winds of change taking place throughout Jamaica as well as the global influences which were touching upon the youth. Ms. White emphasized the entrepreneurial spirit of the leadership team, with its focus on drawing on the human resources of the community, including attorneys, educators, and financial planners, to investigate and seek funding by partnering with agencies such as the Jamaica Development Bank and UNESCO.

Even as she acknowledged how Eurocentric ideals attempted to curtail the development of the society during the colonial period, she emphasized how the strength of the people's desire for a future based on the inheritance of the past has fostered their journey through to the 21st century. "The Charles Town Maroons have shown us that there are alternative approaches to development," she stated. "Every aspect of the community's development points to ideas rooted in culture. From the social to the economic and the political. These are ideas that are different from Western characteristics. The Charles Town Maroons are people initiating change for themselves."

"Those wild negroes, to whom Governor Thickness scathingly referred centuries ago, are exemplary community leaders engaged in sustainable living, responding with creativity to the changing times," she asserted.

"Today, these wild negroes have withstood the test of time, focusing on community consensus building, and working with their people, setting their goals and achieving them. Legal experts from among their ranks have set up the legal rights framework for the continued operation of their community. Keith Lumsden, nephew of the late Frank Lumsden, provides leadership in exploring the competitive advantage of their heritage. The technical team identified resources, made contacts through the system and is investigating the scope for development of an ethno-medicine industry," Ms. White shared with the audience.

Accompong: Fighting in the Name of Justice and Freedom

The roads were treacherous, seeming almost insurmountable for someone like me who had not visited Accompong before. In my heart, though, I knew that it was well worth traveling to the site of a people who had claimed the mountainous landscape and fought to keep it for their people in the name of justice and freedom. The town of Accompong is situated in St. Elizabeth near Maggotty in the foothills of the Cockpit Country, some 20 miles from

Montego Bay and 19 miles from Black River. Once I arrive there I am stunned by the vast outlay of the land. My eyes rest on the primary school, a symbol of knowledge and cultural retentions so central to Maroon culture. (Later, I meet with school children there and they tell me about their culture and how this has shaped their learning in school.) I meet with Colonel Williams, who tells me that there are concentrated efforts to build up the Accompong Basic School of 60 students, 2 to 6 years old. There is also a Primary school, age 6–12. At age 12, students leave the community to go to high school. They go to Aberdeen and Maggotty and the Cockpit Country.

This dynamic celebration of ancient African culture includes street vendors, food stalls, sparkling fire pits roasting up feasts of food, and the throb of human energy; a diversity of people of all races and ethnicities. This is part of the annual Maroon Festival to honour Colonel Cudjoe's birthday as well as the signing of the 1739 peace treaty. It is reported that up to 15,000 visitors attend this celebration each year, coming from all corners of the globe. In addition, busloads of local school children pour in and I am granted the opportunity to meet with many of them and share their perspective of the meaning and value of Maroon culture.

I join the throng of celebrants and march with the spiritual leaders who follow the beat of drums towards the Peace Cave where they pay respect to their Maroon ancestors at this location of the signing of the peace treaty. The Peace Cave is of great significance to the Accompong Maroons as it is the site where Cudjoe met with the British to finalize the terms of peace.

The Kindah Tree

The group then moves on to the Kindah tree, the Mango tree where Maroons leaders held meetings and Cudjoe held deliberations with the British. (Cudjoe died in Nanny Town 5 years after the peace treaty). The ceremony under the mango tree is led by a group of ritualist women who pray to the ancestors and call on their divine presence. As they invoke the spirit of the ancestors, the women are overcome with the spirit. The emotional pitch of their chanting reaches a crescendo, and two of the women convulse in spasms and begin speaking in tongues. The others urge the participants to step out of the way and allow the ancestors to pass into the gathering. "Clear the way. Clear the way. The ancestors are among us. Clear the way," they intone in unison. I am holding onto the Kindah tree, surrounded by hundreds of participants, when I suddenly realize that I am shaking and crying.

This emotionally charged event leads to a march towards the entrance of the village, and I join the throng marching to drumbeats tracing our footsteps back towards the entrance of the village. We reach the flattened pathway and I see a throng of Maroons draped in green plants, entwining their bodies in ritualistic re-enactment of the preparation for battle. The drums beat loud and sonorous, and men and women covered in leaves of the Kindeh tree march an ancient path, dancing and singing, all the while calling on the ancestors for strength, guidance, and protection. The march ends at a covered tent facing a large stage, where Colonel Ferron Williams, Accompong leader, calls the proceedings to order, welcoming the dignitaries and guests. This official acknowledgement, which includes presentations and performances, is followed by feasting, dancing, and traditional myal drumming. The celebration continues all day and culminates at night in a sound-system dance party that continues till the break of dawn. This has been a moving celebration of spiritual culture, music, sacred practices, and the ancient language of the Koromante.

Trelawny Town: Justice, Equality and Mutual Respect

The Maroon communities of Jamaica are renowned for their record of sustaining a community of practice established on the foundation of their African heritage rooted in eco-sustainability. Trelawny Town, the largest of the Maroon communities during slavery, was developed on such a philosophy by its renowned leader Captain Cudjoe, who was born in 1694 and died in 1744 in Nanny Town. Local sources say he was the son of Quateng, a chief from the Koromante people in Ghana, captured and sold into Spanish slavery and brought to Jamaica. He is reputed to have established the first Maroon community after a successful rebellion he led against the plantation system in Jamaica. Captain Cudjoe focused on building a community based on justice, equality, and mutual respect. He was unwavering in his position, especially in dealing with the British. Trelawny Town is known today as Flagstaff, and locals insist that the popular Revivalism religion grew out of Maroon culture here at (Trelawny Town) Flagstaff.

Cudjoe was the chief negotiator with the British following the first Maroon War and the signing of the 1739 peace treaty. Many years of peace followed. However, in 1795 Governor Balcarres decided to wage war on the Maroons using the excuse of some minor breaches of the treaty by the Trelawny Maroons. Three-hundred Maroons fought against 1500 British and 3000 local volunteers for 5 months. The Maroons successfully held sway against the British and both sides came to terms with an accord of peace. The British, however, with a devious plan to renege on the terms, invited the Maroon leaders to a peace celebration dinner at which time they captured the Maroons and banished them to Nova Scotia with the offer of sending them to Sierra Leone. In 1800 most of the Maroons set sail to Sierra Leone, where they became influential, establishing churches and a political system. The British, fearful of the revival of a Maroon presence in Trelawny, wiped out the village and began erecting monuments to their imperial power, including a fort.

Scotts Hall: Indigenous Self-Determination

Scotts Hall is a Maroon settlement located in the interior of St. Mary, established in 1796 after 26 Maroons received permission to migrate from Crawford Town and settle there. These Maroons went on to establish the town based on the guiding principles of the other locations. The town is located close to Wag River in St. Mary, a main source of food, transportation, and resources during times of battle and war with the British. In time, the Windward Maroon court, handling issues for all the settlements, was established here. The Maroon hospital was also erected here, serving all the Maroon communities. Maroons would utilize an underground tunnel to travel from the various locations for medical attention based on their African practices, relying heavily on herbs and healing waters. The economic life of the community is centered on agricultural production—breadfruit, yam, red peas, banana. The annual celebration takes place August 1, with ceremonial dances and ritual enactments embedded within centuries-old practices carried over from slavery through the Maroon Wars and post-emancipation Jamaica.

Scott's Hall is rooted in the region's history of colonialism, warriorship, plantation agriculture, and slavery. The Maroon's presence is a testimony to the people's warriorship and defeat of oppression. Their strength and vitality is reflected in their historical continuity of leadership and culture. Colonel Pinhay presided as chief for 33 years before the current Colonel Rudolph Pink was elected in 2016.

Reflective Conversations: Question! Reflect! Write!

1. In this chapter we have learnt about the Maroons' connection to their African heritage. Work with a group of your peers to create a collage or video that expresses what it means to be a Maroon in the 21st century.
2. How do the children of Moore Town convey their connection to the historical figure of Nanny of the Maroons?
3. What would you consider to be the main difference between the Maroon villages today and the past centuries?

References

Bilby, K. (2005). *True born Maroons*. Orlando, FL: University Press of Florida.

Craton, M. (1982). *Testing the chains: Resistance to slavery in the British West Indies*. Ithaca, NY: Cornell University Press.

Estes, C. P. (1992). *Women who run with the wolves: Myths & legends of the wild woman archetype*. New York, NY: Ballantine Books.

Freire, P. (1970/2007). *Pedagogy of the oppressed*. New York, NY: Continuum.

Jamaica Assembly. (1796). *Proceedings of the Governor & Assembly of Jamaica in regard to the Maroon Negroes. Gale 18th Century Collection*. Nova Southeastern University Law Library. Retrieved July 31, 2014.

Jamaica Information Service. (2014). Nanny of the Maroons. Retrieved from https://jis.gov.jm/information/heroes/nanny-of-the-maroons/

Kocher, R. E. (2002). Revisiting a site of cultural bondage: JoAnn Gibson Robinson's boycott memoir. In Susan Shifrin (Ed), *Women as sites of culture: Women's roles in cultural formation from the Renaissance to the Twentieth Century* (pp. 245–256). Burlington, VT: Ashgate.

Preston, P. (1997). *Political/cultural identity: Citizens and nation in a global era*. London, England: SAGE.

Rucker, W. (2015). *Gold coast diasporas: Identity, culture and power*. Bloomington, IN: Indiana University Press.

Sharpe, J. (2003). *The ghosts of slavery: A literary archeology of black women's lives*. Minneapolis, MN: University of Minnesota Press.

Sherlock, P., & Bennett, H. (1998). *The story of the Jamaican people*. Kingston, Jamaica: Ian Randle.

UNESCO. (2003). *International decade for people of African descent (2015–2024)*. Retrieved from http://en.unesco.org/decade-people-african-descent

· 1 0 ·

AFRICAN CULTURAL RETENTIONS

We refuse to be what you want us to be. We are what we are.

—Bob Marley

Throughout history the Maroons and other Indigenous people have developed rituals and ceremonies to help make sense of the world. For Indigenous people, their life force comes from a connection to earth—outwardly and inwardly—and the accumulated wisdom of their lineage passing down from one generation to the next. We find these traces residing within New World African religious practices, for example, which invoke—by means of music, dance, and trance—the ancestral spirits as well as the collective memories of important events and people. The centrality of these ritual performances attests to the fact that both a historical memory and an artistic sensibility have played an important role for Africans in maintaining, elaborating, and creating their worldviews, identity, and lifeways (Stolzoff, 2000, p.14).

From their example, we have the blueprint to create a community of practice that reaches across borders and offers innovative ways of thinking about belonging. These are role models who inspire us to begin our own inquiries. We can draw upon their spirit and philosophy to deepen critical encounters with the literacy we experience today in contemporary class-rooms and global communities, albeit with new tools, including the Web and digital technology.

Oral Traditions

Oral traditions have been our way of telling our stories and passing down traditions of a rich, powerful, and enduring legacy. For thousands of years, the continent of Africa has been home to many economically rich, socially advanced, and culturally varied civilizations. When the Europeans came to the region looking for gold and riches, they mistook the continent's lack of written language tradition as an indication that the people and their way of life were primitive.

Nanny and the other Africans carried with them these centuries of rich cultural legacy, which they transplanted within the context and circum-stances which gave them agency and communal identity. Nanny and the Maroons played a significant role in maintaining the culture and traditions of the Motherland through music, dance, spiritual practices, cultural artifacts, and language. In gaining their sovereignty, the Maroons became culturally rooted in the land and created an eco-Indigenous community which stands as a pillar in the region and the world.

Spiritual and Military Leadership: An Enduring Community of Practice

The substance of Nanny's heroism is recognized throughout the African New World Diaspora. She is held in high esteem for the attitude that led to the building of a Maroon community with the resiliency to work actively to transform challenges into opportunities. She stands out as an iconic figure in Maroon historiography. The heroine who was intent on securing and main-taining freedom; who worked with her brothers to set about establishing a community of practice based on freedom and integrity, with guerilla warfare as their tool. She is known as one of the earliest leaders of slave resistance in the Americas, and one of very few women. The spiritual, cultural, and mili-tary leader of the Maroons, she is highly esteemed for her remarkable accom-plishments; a key figure in the political framework of the Maroon leadership and resistance in the Americas. Her sustained resistance against the British absorbed their attention, and the recognition that they faced a formidable foe that they could not conquer. Both recorded history and folk narrative emphasize that Nanny did not agree with a peace treaty and was prepared to continue fighting the British. However, she gave her support to Cudjoe in the signing of the 1739 peace treaty. As the community storytellers recount it, the agreement to desist from raiding plantations and returning runaway slaves was only a political move as Nanny and the other Maroons continued stealthily with their subversive acts.

Militant and nurturing, Nanny exuded such a dynamic force that her followers felt they were well supported by the Ashanti West African supreme god, Nyankypon, who blessed them in their assertion of the right to liberty. She created a formidable team with her brothers Cudjoe, Accompong, Johnny, Cuffy, and Quao. Gabriel (2004) noted, for example, that the notorious slave owner, Thickness, recounted his encounter with her in his 1788 journal: "the old hag had a girdle around her waist with nine or ten different knives hanging in sheaths to it, many of which I have no doubt have been plunged in human flesh and blood."

Standing Up to Imperialism

The metaphor of the Maroons as David standing up to the giant of Imperialism is an apt one which may serve to reinforce for youth the value of standing up against bias and injustice. *"From time to time, without the leaft provocation and by their barbarities and outrage intimidated the whites"* (Jamaica Assembly, 1796). It is of value to locate stories of such groups who acted as agents of change by drawing upon their own cultural capital to contest dominant power relations (Giroux, 1996). Comments such as this and others in the parliamentary proceedings suggest that the British harbored a deep fear of the Maroons; a fear which no doubt propelled the negotiations for the peace treaty. This is an example of a community of practice that may be shared across borders to offer innovative ways of thinking about belonging, engendering symbolic and ideological momentum. Their existence today remains a challenge to the colonial legacy of British imperialism. The knowledge of their achievements rings around the region to inspire social legitimacy and cultural confidence. This is a community that reflects economic development, stability, and methods of sustainability as well as governance and political empowerment. These warriors of history demanded freedom from the oppressors, knowing, as Martin Luther King stated, *it would not be voluntarily given*. It is amazing to note how they forged a community of culture and politics which remains intact today, upholding African cultural retentions.

In addition, the post-colonial narratives of resistance and empowerment of Nanny of the Maroons are great examples to highlight the possibilities of women in politics, especially for children of diverse cultures and working-class backgrounds. These stories suggest strategies to dismantle structures that constrain women in building their capacity to actualize their dreams, connecting the need to be resolute in the 21st century to the same resolve and commitment that Nanny exemplified in the 18th century. Gaaman (Mama G) stresses the relevance of the legend of Nanny in 21st century discourse as one that stimulates the imagination and transports us to that revolutionary world of our brave ancestors. She emphasizes the political power wielded by Nanny as the community respected her as both military leader and ritualist specialist with an expertise in herbal healing and obeah. Nanny's influence, she asserts, exerts a powerful force in today's society and has spread throughout the region, empowering other women to become community leaders and ritual specialists. She speaks to the efficacy of the obeah woman in African spirituality heritage and the central role she must play in healing historical violence, yet she is still decried in the society. She states that the story of Nanny grants wisdom and guidance to the communities of Caribbean women to counteract domestic violence and poverty. She speaks of the ancient tradition of hand sewing which is used to help heal those who have been exposed to violence. "I have to sound that abeng!" she declares, speaking metaphorically of this sacred artifact.

Gaaman Gloria Simms reflects,
The power of our community lies in the power of our ancestors. We women, have a special responsibility not just to uplift ourselves but to pull up everyone around us regardless of the circumstances we face. We do not have a choice.

Gaaman is the first female in the history of the Maroons to be crowned Queen. She emphasizes the communal belonging that is central to Maroon ideology. "This spirit of community," she stresses, "has served to hold us together across the ages, as people whose destiny is linked to Africa." Surinamese Ambassador Fidelia Graand-Galon speaks of Nanny's strength and the way it ripples through the region "to connect us all together."

Ideology of Resistance

Accompong, Scott's Hall, Moore Town (Nanny Town), and Trelawny Town are cultural models of communities defending a culture and a way of life. These Maroon villages highlight the power of place, the forging of a community of practice. However, the value of cultural material as classroom resource is under-explored and underrepresented in the literature used in schools (Apple, 1996; Bhabha, 1994; Kanu, 2006). These stories provide the texts that explore the trans-national and trans-colonial links across the Americas. Within the Caribbean Diaspora, they become the alternative history texts of narratives of slavery, resistance, and emancipation; alternative realities that we have to ensure become part of the broader canon and material that youth have access to. How we negotiate our relationship within the broader community owes much to the social, historical, and political lens through which we filter these stories; our cultural narratives. Stories are integral to our identity. They provide us with a blueprint to question forms of power, privilege, and inequity. The stories of the Maroons of Jamaica have played a central role in the shaping of identity nationwide even as they have emboldened the descendants and provided them with tools of cultural retentions that have worked to shape them into autonomous units within the Jamaican society. Nanny succored strength from the ideology of her people to resist European imperialism. Along with her warriors, she transformed the colonialist-imposed identity of race-inherent inferiority to become a thorn in the side of the British, forcing them to negotiate a ceasefire as evidenced by the 1739 peace treaties (Gabriel, 2004).

Connecting Globally Through Storytelling

Storytelling, a central part of oral tradition, has always been a vital resource for diverse people who have relied on this essential tool throughout the ages to maintain the integrity of their cultural heritage. Myths, like other forms of storytelling, were developed to explain a people's world, how they came to be, and their place in the universe. Indeed, a country's stories and myths provide a striking confirmation of the essence of its vision of itself and of the world, and especially, the future of its young. Through memory-keeping and storytelling we are able to counter the discontinuity of our history and traditions that Euro-centrism has sought to impose on us. These have proven to be effective strategies to bring the generations together and perpetuate our culture. Our stories enable us to travel in many directions, through metaphors and symbols, and to connect with a world beyond the narrow confines of geography and man-made boundaries.

Grassroots Leadership

Maroon agency is a significant portrayal of the possibilities of leadership from the bottom up, and as such has implications for curriculum leadership at school sites by educators who would dare to take risks. It confronts the aftermath of the colonial state with the presence to channel resources to mitigate the uneven effects of historical inequality (Mair, 1974/2006).

From the Maroon communities, I have discerned seven basic tenets of establishing and maintaining a community of practice:

1. Celebrate human existence.
2. Nurture the indomitable will of the human spirit.
3. Resist the thrust of individualism.
4. Celebrate human dignity and rights.
5. Participate in transformative rituals.
6. Respect and live in unity with the communal land.
7. Embed cultural retentions within the structural framework of the community.

The combination of all seven elements enabled the Maroons to exert strategies of resistance to disrupt the Eurocentric traditions and revolutionize their socio-political communities (Ashcroft, Griffiths, & Tiffin, 1989). This is a significant step in dismantling the hierarchical order and the patriarchy that has held sway over post-colonial societies such as Jamaica. This community resisted the fragmentation intended by colonialism (Ashcroft et al., 1989) to maintain their historical registers. Maroon historiography is emblematic of the self-reliance and independence that sustain individuals and build communities (Agorsah, 1994). Through their practices they are reflecting themes relevant to the marginalized worldwide. Their story is about struggle, triumph, worship, family; the building of a community of practice against all odds. The cultural heritage they have preserved is a developmental resource that extends beyond the borders of their community into the entire Jamaica and the Diaspora. Portia Simpson, former Prime Minister of Jamaica, and the only woman to have held this position, constantly provoked her people and at times created unease with the question, "What could there be that we, their heirs can't do today?"

Rising up from a local marginalized community through the political ranks with its inherent competition and patriarchal relationships, the Honorable Portia Simpson highlighted to the Jamaican and global community the very model of grassroots innovation that I connect to the foundation of Freirean philosophy of problem-posing and problem-solving processes that seek to make visible power dynamics and address inequitable conditions (Freire, 1970/2007). Inherent in the story of Nanny of the Maroons and the parallels that can be drawn with Portia Simpson who publicly claimed Nanny as her heroine is the ideology that grassroots leadership is often resolute in its commitment to disrupt and dismantle hegemony. Other Caribbean female leaders, such as Eugenia Charles, Kamla Persad-Bissessar, and Cécile La Grenade have demonstrated a similar agency as they work to establish creative and transformative leadership. Like Nanny, they have shattered borders and interrupted the hegemonic construct of power in their societies and contributed to the winds of change across the Americas.

Nanny is a prototype for leadership in communities seeking transformation. I call on the story of Nanny to demonstrate how her agency for change has disrupted the status quo and altered the landscape of history and politics in the Diaspora. Her legend became so powerful that it was reputed that she caught the British musket balls in her anus and fired them back at her enemies. When her community was on the brink of starvation, she planted seeds gifted her by her ancestors from which pumpkins flourished and fed the entire community. She is remembered as a critical thinker who retreated to Dinner Mountain to reflect and plan her strategies of guerilla warfare and the leadership of her people. The legends include stories of her actions of reflection and renewal, where she spent time in solitude to ponder the condition of her people and gather spiritual resources to confront the British. She cultivated the capacity for tolerating stillness and creating spaciousness of the soul.

In exploring this graphic image of reflexivity, pulled from the intergenerational archives of Maroonage, I position it as a metaphor, a paradigm of the African cultural retentions in the New World. This metaphor elevates the value of dreaming to envision a better world, to seek to shift perspective and foster an intellectual climate that becomes a third space where Black and White, Indigenous and non-Indigenous folk meet to investigate the meaning of inclusion, collaboration, and achievement.

This theme of the value of the oral tradition among Indigenous people continues to resonate throughout my work and I am inspired to continue the exploration of the ways in which this feminist freedom-fighter, Nanny of the Maroons, has contributed to the sense of self- determination and, ultimately, identity. Everything points to the need to continue with the collaborative inquiry and the methodological explorations into resistance and empowerment across Indigenous communities worldwide. Indeed, international collaboration is a significant part to the change patterns of classroom discourse and gives consideration to how reflective processes and practices developed by the teacher research and inquiry movements could be channeled toward improving student learning and ultimately obtaining more equitable outcomes for students. Writing ourselves into history must begin with an examination of where we are and who we are. We must seize qualitative tools to write ourselves into history knowing full well that while there is legitimacy to the historical, anthropological, and ethnographic contributions to the scholarship, we, Indigenous people, must tell our stories ourselves, for no one else can adequately convey the impact of colonization on the Indigenous persona, how the Indigenous spirit has been fostered, and the ways in which it must gain expression. It is this act of ancestral writing that will lead to the creation of a pedagogy of hope especially for our youth.

Reflective Conversations: Question! Reflect! Write!

1. Most people are fascinated by human nature. They like to know how other people respond to problems, disappointments, and temptations. Identify one aspect of Maroon life that reveals something important about human nature. Write to express this idea and share your reason for selecting this example.

2. Imagine that you are Nanny of the Maroons. Write a single journal entry of a day in your life when you had to deal with an issue affecting the community. What was the issue? How did you handle it?

3. How have 21st-century Maroons been able to sustain the various forms of cultural expression and safeguard and perpetuate their cultural legacy? How are they able to make a contribution to the broader cultural, social, and political landscape of their country, Jamaica, and perhaps the global community?

References

Apple, M. (1996). *Cultural politics and education*. New York, NY: Teachers College Press.

Agorsah, E.K. (1994). *Maroon Heritage: Archaeological, Ethnographic and Historical Perspectives*. Oak Park, Illinois: Canoe Press.

Ashcroft, B., Griffiths, G., & Tiffin, H. (1999). *Key concepts in post-colonial studies*. London, England; New York, NY: Routledge.

Bhabha, H. (1994). *The location of culture*. London, England: Routledge.

Freire, P. (1970/2007). Pedagogy of the oppressed. New York: Continuum.

Gabriel, D. (2004). Jamaica's true Queen: Nanny of the Maroons. Retrieved from https://jamaicans.com/queennanny/

Giroux, H. (1996). Resisting difference: Cultural studies and the discourse of critical pedagogy. In L. Grossberg, C. Nelson, & P. Treichler (Eds.), *Cultural studies* (pp.199–212). New York, NY: Routledge.

Jamaica Assembly. (1796). *Proceedings of the Governor & Assembly of Jamaica in regard to the Maroon Negroes*. Gale 18th Century Collection. Nova Southeastern University Law Library. Retrieved July 31, 2014.

Kanu, Y. (2006). *Curriculum as cultural practice*. Toronto, Canada: University of Toronto Press.

Mair, M. (1974/2006). *A historical study of women in Jamaica*. Kingston, Jamaica: University of the West Indies Press.

Stolzoff, N. (2000). *Wake the town and tell the people: Dancehall culture in Jamaica*. Durham, NC: Duke University Press.

POSTSCRIPT

Writing Truth into History

Nanny of the Maroons: Political Icon
of the African Diaspora

The way the residents of the Maroon communities tell it, Maroon life is empowering. Having only opened up their communities to non-citizens in 1986, the Maroons have remained isolated within the interior of the Jamaican mountain landscape for centuries. The pristine landscape, the fresh air, the absence of the din of capitalism, the community of brotherhood, the safety, and the spiritual connection with Nature are all elements of a way of life that is different from the rest of the country and most capitalist societies. This concept of communal support, each one helping the other, has been the foundation of Maroon community. Within this era of social and political instability, the Maroons are a living story of how communities thrive. As societies across the globe struggle with handling the ways in which capitalism impacts our capacity to have a just society and an equitable educational system, the Maroons' way of life may provide us with some directions. Metaphorically, the image of Nanny looms large within this landscape. Nanny was a critical thinker and problem-solver whose actions left a legacy of lessons in perseverance. The substance of Nanny's experience leads to a significant contribution to the shaping of the West Indian identity and the bequeathing of a cultural legacy that transcends borders to inform the mind and spirit of a people with the knowledge that they have an inherited legacy infused with the wisdom of their ancestors on which to draw. Her story shows the complex and circuitous path, including her relationship with Cudjoe and her other brothers, which led her to the esteemed position of Queen Nanny, leader of the Windward Maroons. She and the other Maroons tapped into the crucible of their heritage to fashion the meagre resources available to them to produce abundant results. As a historical figure she stood up to the violence of slavery and resisted and thus is symbolic of the fighting spirit of humans who refuse to be subjugated by their circumstances. Alienated and cut off from the land of her birth, she examined the available resources of her location and organized how to use them effectively by bridging the past with her present circumstances. As an example, she demonstrates that tapping into one's potential creates a continuum for creativity; working cooperatively with others; facing challenges; and mending the way as you move along on the journey.

Sixty years after nine Black students integrated schools in the southern United States, we continue to confront racism within the educational system as well as the broader society. At the time of writing in 2017, the United States, deemed the world's most developed country, continues to reveal deep chasms in its social structure; a divisiveness fostered by racism and the entrenched desire by White supremacists to maintain the status quo. The classroom narratives in this text point to how teachers of all backgrounds can engage children in multicultural literature and critical-pedagogy-initiating classroom practices and curricula that embrace a social justice and equity agenda. In such a classroom, space is created for diverse forms of knowledge to be accepted, including Indigenous Knowledge Epistemology. My students have demonstrated their interest in global literature and revealed their growth in historical consciousness. Within the scope of the cultural space we created together, they negotiated multiple cultural locations, including their own background, and created new forms of knowledge.

They investigated the power of story in their own lives; stories that reflect their beliefs, cultural identity, vocabulary, and language originating from their family. As the school year evolved, their historical consciousness developed and they were able to make connections between our classroom pedagogy and historical developments. They learned about human perseverance and gained priceless insight into the value of the environment. These are themes that are of great significance in classroom instruction in the lives of both student and teacher, encouraging us to be active participants in the story we are living; not bystanders, but historically conscious individuals who may be inspired to become agents of change.

My collaboration with international scholars has highlighted our shared spirituality and historical legacy. As Indigenous scholars we have been hungry for intellectual exchange and space to share our unique history from a multi-faceted perspective. We have been able to interrogate our current challenges as we work together on our collaborative journey. Our coming together on Maroon land emphasized our ability to transcend coloniality. Despite geographic distances, the complex negotiations of local, trans-national identities and cultural identities, I have benefitted from the collaboration with Indigenous colleagues across the globe and I bring this awareness into the cultural space of the classroom.

> *What impedes our capacity to make meaningful change? What is the value of the century of educational research we have conducted? Is there anything in the research that points to the way we can balance the ideology of American individualism with the communal consciousness of Indigenous people?*

Although these pressing questions have emerged from my investigation of the Jamaican Maroons, I believe that I can echo the lyrics of Bob Marley and encourage teachers, leaders, young women, and women of my generation with the admonition, "No, no woman no cry," for we have the multidisciplinary tools in our grasp, and we can succor the courage to engage with the world in relation to historical, geo-political, and protest and intellectual movements such as Black Lives Matter and SOS Blak Australia. The story of Nanny as an empowered woman disrupts the status quo and provides fresh insights into the resistance movement during and after slavery. A representative of female autonomy; a messenger heralding the future, her spiritual and familial influence asserts a strong influence throughout the African Diaspora. She is a metaphor that can be used to offer direction and guidance for teaching in classrooms in Jamaica, the Caribbean, and across the globe. Nanny and the Jamaican Maroons are telling a different story from the Eurocentric meta-narrative, offering alternative perspectives of the history and legacies of the transatlantic slave trade. In observing the results of their intellectual, spiritual, and ideological resistance the Maroon villages reminded me that a world of justice is possible, and I have been able to access tools and materials that have fostered my work with children in schools. From this social-justice-oriented learning, both my students and I have achieved great clarity of understanding the socio-political ideology of resistance to hegemony.

INDEX

www.ingramcontent.com/pod-product-compliance
Lightning Source LLC
Chambersburg PA
CBHW050610280326
41932CB00016B/2982